The Laurel Shakespeare

Each play is presented in a separate volume handsomely designed to incorporate these special features:

THE TEXT is a modern restoration of the original folios completed in late 1957 by *Charles Jasper Sisson*, Assistant Director and Senior Fellow at the Shakespeare Institute, Stratford-upon-Avon.

THE FORMAT designed for this volume employs the largest and most readable type available in any popular edition of the plays.

THE MODERN COMMENTARY by actors, directors and critics recently associated with the respective plays offers an authoritative insight into a special aspect of the play. *Margaret Webster* toured the United States with her production of THE TAMING OF THE SHREW after World War II.

THE INTRODUCTION by the General Editor, *Francis Fergusson,* University Professor of Comparative Literature at Rutgers, provides dramatic and critical background.

SHAKESPEARE AND HIS THEATRE, also by *Professor Fergusson*, presents the known facts of Shakespeare's life and dramatic career along with a description of the Globe company.

THE GLOSSARY, especially prepared for this volume by *H. H. Smith,* Princeton University, defines Elizabethan terms and special allusions not found in desk dictionaries.

The Laurel Shakespeare
Francis Fergusson, General Editor

The Taming
of the Shrew

by William Shakespeare

Text edited by Charles Jasper Sisson

Commentary by Margaret Webster

Published by
DELL PUBLISHING CO., INC.
750 Third Avenue
New York 17, N. Y.

Cover design by Jerome Kuhl

Frontispiece drawing by Paul Wenck after
the Droeshout engraving in the First Folio

Produced by Western Printing &
Lithographing Company

First printing—April, 1958
Second printing—September, 1958

Printed in U.S.A.

CONTENTS

Introduction by the General Editor

Shakespeare had in all probability written *The Taming of the Shrew* by 1592, when he was twenty-eight. It is one of his earliest surviving plays, and (by his standards) the work of a beginner. But he seems to have known, even then, exactly what he wished to do: to make a scenario which the actors could use as the framework for an evening's hilarious entertainment. He succeeded far better than he could have hoped to do. *The Shrew* has held the stage (as Dame Margaret Webster points out in her Director's Comments) ever since he wrote it. It appears on the contemporary stage frequently, and with success, in productions and adaptations of every description. It is one of the easiest and most "surefire" of his plays, for good actors know instinctively how to handle its quick, clear succession of farcical situations, and the reader can enjoy it at once, and interpret it according to his own taste.

Because it is basically so clear and simple, it can be understood and judged in various ways. Those who come to it from a reading of Shakespeare's later comedies sometimes find it lacking in subtlety, even cruel and vulgar. But it is beloved in the theatre, and some critics, including Dr. Johnson and Hazlitt, have given it their august approval. Shakespeare made it out of three quite different stories. The central plot is that of Bianca, her rich father, Baptista Minola, and her three suitors. Shakespeare added to this plot the story of "Kate the curst" and her energetic suitor Petruchio, by making Kate the elder daughter, who must be married before Bianca. The "Induction," in which the drunken Tinker, Christopher Sly, is kidnaped for an evening of luxury and invited to see *The Taming of the Shrew,* is from a third source. In the play as we have it all these elements fuse naturally together to make an evening's entertainment. But one can understand the possibilities in the script better

—and the disagreements of the critics—if one remembers
Shakespeare's variegated sources. It was always his custom
to use familiar tales for the plots of his plays. In *The Shrew*
his characteristic method can be seen more clearly than in
the later and more mysterious plays.

We usually assume that the comedy is simply about Petruchio's violent wooing of Kate—and with good reason, for
their affair gives the play its title and attracts the crowd
generation after generation. The problem of taming a wife
is as old, laughable, and insoluble as death and taxes. It can
be found in European literature in many versions, several
of which Shakespeare might have known. One of them is a
popular tale in doggerel verse called "A Merry Jest of a
Shrewd and Curst Wife Lapped in Morel's Skin, for her
Good Behaviour." It is very crude, but lively, and illuminating as a specimen of uninhibited popular humor shortly
before Shakespeare's time. The fun depends almost entirely
upon the physical struggles between the man and his domi-
neering wife, and the effect is bawdy and brutal—when the
husband finally wins, he flays his wife and wraps her in the
salted hide of his old horse "Morel." It has been conjectured
that this was Shakespeare's immediate source for Katharine
and Petruchio; but if so he completely transformed it, shift-
ing the interest to the human relation between the two.
Some of the old violence still shows through in unimagina-
tive productions, and Shakespeare no doubt counted on the
elementary basis of the squabble to add "salt" and excite-
ment. But his Katharine and Petruchio, though lightly
sketched, already suggest his own humane and balanced
vision.

Shakespeare sees Katharine and Petruchio as in love, almost from the first meeting. Their fights are partly a flirta-
tious game, partly a matter of egoism, male and female,
with a good deal of bluffing on both sides. Katharine is perhaps testing Petruchio, hoping half-consciously that he will
survive her impossible stunts and thereby prove to be the
husband she requires. Petruchio accepts the challenge with
relish; we feel some love and insight in him even as he roars

at the terrible Katharine, starves her, and tramples on her tender vanities. At the end of the play, when both are for the moment exhausted, Katharine gives her famous speech on wifely duty. There is plenty of irony in this speech—which no husband in the audience can miss—but there is gratitude too. Katharine has wakened from her nightmare of the bad little girl; she has grown up; the strenuous game has, for the moment at least, a happy ending.

It has often been pointed out that Katharine and Petruchio foreshadow Beatrice and Benedick in *Much Ado about Nothing,* Shakespeare's final word on the battles of the egoistic young in love. But in that play he lifts the theme to the most poetic high-comedy, whereas in *The Shrew* he sticks to the mood and style of farce. The play should be read, as well as performed, with that style in mind. Petruchio, for instance, may be heard roaring offstage, and then appear cracking a ten-foot bullwhip (as Mr. Pernell Roberts did in the production of The American Shakespeare Festival at Stratford, Connecticut); the effect is hilarious, not brutal, because the style is right. The whip shows (with overemphasis) how Petruchio feels; but it is no more frightening than the firecrackers in the circus that blow the clowns twenty feet in all directions—after which they all get up and run away. Such is the magic of the best popular farce of all ages and countries.

The whole play of *The Shrew* owes a great deal to farce of this kind, which the young Shakespeare knew in Latin, French, and especially Italian sources; much lighter and drier entertainment than native British humor like "A Merry Jest." The main plot, that of Bianca and her suitors, is a typical Latin comedy of "intrigue"—a game for the girl, or the money, or both. The characters are lightly sketched as familiar types; the situations are obvious and universal; the point is neither psychology nor feeling, but wit, and the absurd complexities of the plot. Baptista wants to marry off his daughters as richly and speedily as possible; Lucentio wants Bianca; Hortensio wants her money; and Gremio wants to warm his old bones with a young

wife. On this earthy basis all the arabesques of the intrigue
are built, including the improbable disguises of Lucentio
and Hortensio as Pedants, the exchanges of clothes between
master and man, and the rest. Shakespeare took the Bianca
story directly or indirectly from Gascoigne's "The Supposes," a translation of Ariosto's Italian comedy, "Gli
Suppositi." Ariosto in turn had derived his play from two
Latin comedies, one by Terence and one by Plautus. Ariosto's play is swifter and more intelligent than his Latin
models, and Gascoigne's English version preserves some of
that sophistication. It was performed with success for the
alert and well-educated young gentlemen–law students at
Gray's Inn, and Shakespeare would have known of it as a
rather special hit of a past season. When he combined it
with the Induction and the Katharine-Petruchio story to
make *The Shrew,* he transformed it and made it his own.
Some of his touches of characterization suggest his later
(and very un-Latin) style. And he was thinking, not of the
small cultivated audience, but of the popular audience of
the public theatres; he was moving toward his own, English,
"romantic" kind of comedy. He was not moving toward the
art of Molière, who two generations later was to bring the
Latin comic style to its ultimate perfection. *The Shrew,* in
short, is unmistakably Shakespeare; but like the other very
early comedies, *Two Gentlemen of Verona* and *The Comedy of Errors,* it is his reworking of a Latin source.

He stressed the Italian flavor, perhaps as a way of adding
to the fun, or in order to make the whole absurd tangle of
the plot acceptable to a London crowd. Petruchio's name is
spelled incorrectly for Italian, but in such a way as to indicate for the English reader the correct Italian pronuncia-
tion. The play abounds in little touches apparently intended
to evoke an Italian atmosphere: old Gremio's description
of his rich-merchant's house; references to Italian towns;
details of Italian university life; pedantic tag-ends of Latin,
and a few Italian phrases of politeness. Gremio is called "A
Pantalowne"—a reference to a character in the Commedia
dell' Arte, the Italian vaudeville or improvised comedy of

the time. That character appears in countless pictures of the Commedia as *Pantalone,* the rich old Venetian who is always chasing young girls with grotesque and single-minded agility. On the bare platform-stage of Shakespeare's theatre very little of the Italian locale would have been represented in actual settings. The costumes might have been vaguely Italian, and perhaps also the properties used for such effects as the final wedding-feast. But the chief value of the Italian flavor is to suggest a playing-style. The actors appear at the end of the Induction as actors, so that when they leap into their roles as Kate, Petruchio, and the rest we know—like the bleary Sly who watches them onstage—that it is all in fun. In our time vaudeville, very light opera, and the best circus clowning continue this style of playing.

The third story which Shakespeare used to make the play is of course that of Sly, the lovable drunk of the Induction. Here too Shakespeare was relying on old and well-tried materials. The device of beginning a play with an induction was itself familiar and popular. The story of a penniless and drunken citizen who (for a practical joke, or to make a parable of human vanity) is treated for one night as a nobleman rich enough to satisfy his every desire, is in *The Arabian Nights,* as well as in later versions which Shakespeare might have known. But Christopher Sly himself is strictly Shakespeare's, a creation almost as inspired as Katharine herself. There is nothing Italian about Sly: much of his charm lies in his familiar, homey innocence. He is the first in the long line of Shakespearean clowns, including Bottom the Weaver in *A Midsummer Night's Dream,* Dogberry in *Much Ado,* even Caliban himself in *The Tempest*—all of whom live with the mysterious, sad, and laughable poetry of the dim-witted. Sly is worth having on any terms, a juicy morsel for actor and audience. But it is a little uncertain (in the text of the play as we have it) just how Shakespeare intended to relate Sly to the rest of the evening's entertainment.

Did Shakespeare intend to frame the whole story of *The Shrew* within Sly's comic and touching adventure? It was his custom to begin and end his comedies with poetry or music. *The Comedy of Errors* begins and ends with the nostalgic theme of long-lost sons and brothers. *Twelfth Night* ends with Feste's beautiful and wistful song, "When that I was and a tiny little boy." There are many other examples; and the principle at work here is sound "theatre": the best way to end a farce is to change the mood, and send the audience home relaxed, and a bit sentimental. In his early comedies Shakespeare may have followed this principle by instinct and theatre custom, like modern producers of reviews and musicals, but when he gained fully conscious control of the theatre, he used the musical ending to convey some gently ironic comment of his own upon the deluded human animal. Sly's episode, light and brief as it is, is so good that one may be tempted to think that it foreshadows Shakespeare's later practice. The huntsman-lord who plays the joke on Sly reminds one of Theseus, in *A Midsummer Night's Dream,* with his musical hounds. The whole notion of a play-within-a-play is used in Shakespeare's later work to suggest the dreamlike quality both of the play and of human life itself. And one of the possible sources of the Sly episode is a very similar tale called (in one version) "The Waking Man's Dreame," in which this notion is expressed as follows: "Vanities, delights, riches, pleasures, and all are past and gone: are they not dreames? . . . All that is actual on this great Theatre of the whole world, when it is ended, differs in nothing from what hath been acted on a Players' stage." Perhaps Shakespeare had that in mind when he wrote Sly; perhaps he had it in mind twenty years later when he wrote, in *The Tempest,*

> We are such stuff
> As dreams are made on; and our little life
> Is rounded with a sleep.

In short, Shakespeare may have planned to present the whole farce of *The Shrew* from Sly's point of view, as a joke soon ended, a brief holiday from the daily world we know.

But if that was his intention we should expect to see Sly again at the end, and in the text we have, Sly disappears in the first act. Did Shakespeare bring him back in some earlier version, to let us know that the "dream" of the play was over? Or did he rely on Katharine's final monologue to dispel the mood of farce and return us to the sadder and wiser human world? A good actress, who felt the new tenderness in Kate's relation to Petruchio, could certainly use that final monologue, ironic as it is, for that purpose. But we cannot be sure what Shakespeare wanted to do with Sly after the first act; and on that unanswered question hang a number of disputed minor textual problems. There are also the practical problems which the director must face in staging the play, and these are discussed by Dame Margaret Webster in her Comments.

In *The Taming of the Shrew* we can see Shakespeare, more clearly than in the later plays, as he makes his theatre-magic: seeing the perennial human meaning in old, familiar stories, and weaving them together with his uncanny understanding of his stage, his actors, and his audience. *The Shrew* is put together with far less poetic unity than the comedies of his later phase, but it shows, already, his theatrical mastery. Its interwoven stories, different though they appear in their sources, are all in the main line of popular tales and jokes and theatre. They make a play which comic actors of all kinds, from the most simple-minded to the most sophisticated, can rely on to bring out the best that is in them—and which the reader can enjoy and interpret according to his own taste.

F.F.

SUGGESTIONS FOR FURTHER READING

This play has attracted less critical attention than the later comedies and the great tragedies. It is discussed in Van Doren's *Shakespeare* and Goddard's *The Meaning of Shake-*

speare, listed under "Suggestions for Further Reading on Shakespeare and His Theatre" (page 181). It has not yet appeared in *The New Variorum Shakespeare.*

Collier, J. P. and Hazlitt, W. C. *Shakespeare's Library.* London: 1875.
Volume VI contains *The Taming of a Shrew,* the play, mentioned in the Director's Comment, that has the Sly scenes not included in the accepted text. Modern opinion takes it as a degenerate version of Shakespeare's play, rather than a source.
Volume IV, Part I, contains "Vanity of the World," "The Waking Man's Dreame," and "A Merry Jest of a Shrewd and Curst Wife," conjectural sources mentioned in the Introduction.

Chief Pre-Shakespearean Dramas. Joseph Quincy Adams, editor. New York: 1924.
The best general collection of English plays before Shakespeare. Contains Gascoigne's "The Supposes," the main source of the plot of *The Shrew,* and several comedies which illustrate popular taste before Shakespeare.

Early Plays from the Italian. Edited, with Essay, Introductions and Notes, by R. Warwick Bond. Oxford: 1921.
This study throws much light on Shakespeare's Italian heritage, especially as it influenced *The Shrew.*

Nicoll, Allardyce. *Masks, Mimes and Miracles.* London: 1931.
A standard work on the popular theatre from the Greeks to the eighteenth century. It contains an account of the Commedia dell' Arte, and on pages 346-347 a consideration of its possible influences on Shakespeare. Many good illustrations.

Johnson on Shakespeare. Essays and Notes Selected and Set Forth with an Introduction by Walter Raleigh. Oxford: 1915.

Contains Johnson's Note on *The Shrew*.

Agate, James E. *Brief Chronicles. Shakespeare in Actual Performance.* London: 1943.

The famous English critic writes a rather scornful review of a London production of *The Shrew*.

Narrative and Dramatic Sources of Shakespeare. Edited by Geoffrey Bullough. Vol. I: *Early Comedies, Poems, Romeo and Juliet.* New York and London: 1957.

Contains *The Taming of a Shrew*, an analogue of the Sly episode from Goulart's collection, and Gascoigne's "The Supposes." The editor's introduction summarizes recent scholarly opinion on the probable sources of the play.

A NOTE ON THE TEXT

The text of *The Taming of the Shrew* rests upon the Folio of 1623, which for the first time prints an authorized text. The pirated Quarto, on the other hand, gives a more continuous version of the Induction. In the Folio text, Sly disappears after Act I. Sc. 1, but in the Quarto he is present throughout and gives the epilogue. Elsewhere, too, the Quarto occasionally seems to supply gaps in the Folio text. The editor is bound to follow the authorized text, even if it means losing Sly's epilogue, except where the Quarto's help seems essential in the main dialogue. The Folio text bears signs of alteration and revision, and is generally not without difficulties.

In doubtful readings, the following have been adopted, or introduced: *Ind.* i. 17, Breathe; *Ind.* i. 64, he is Sly; *Ind.* ii. 140, comonty; I. i. 32, checks; I. ii. 112, rhetricks; II. i. 190, all Kates; III. ii. 15, He'll woo as husband; III. ii. 30, Master, master, old news! And such news; III. ii. 49, hipped —with . . . kindred—; III. ii. 130, But sir, to love; III. ii. 211, No, nor tomorrow—not; IV. i. 145, Food, food, food, food!; V. ii. 128, a hundred; V. ii. 148, maintenance.

In accordance with common usage the numbering of lines, together with Act and Scene indications, follows as closely as possible that of the Globe edition. Where no stage directions in fact occur, this is indicated by square brackets enclosing the stage directions.

Spelling is modernized. But there is no modernization of the language as used by Shakespeare and his actors. The elaborate apparatus of stage-directions, mostly dating from eighteenth-century editors, is eschewed. Where the original texts convey Shakespeare's own directions, of course they must be respected, though not necessarily verbatim.

Professor Sisson has further revised the text of this edition.

A Director's Comments on Staging
"The Taming of the Shrew"

BY MARGARET WEBSTER

The Taming of the Shrew (on paper anyway) has been a good deal abused—not entirely without reason. The main plot is "coarse" and "brutal" and the sub-plot "artificial." Even in the playhouse Pepys wrote of it: "It hath some very good pieces in it but generally is but a mean play." Yet so fastidious a critic as Hazlitt thought it "almost the only one of Shakespeare's comedies that has a regular plot and downright moral. It is full of bustle, animation and rapidity of action." Certainly the play or its derivatives have never ceased to hold the stage.

From the Restoration to the middle of the nineteenth century various pirated versions supplanted the original. Garrick's one-act adaptation, *Katherine and Petruchio*, was the most popular. In 1844 Ben Webster, great-grandfather of the present writer, produced the entire play, Induction and all, without scenery and with Sly on the stage. But this bold experiment was a century or so ahead of its time; and when the actor-managers of the nineties and nineteen-hundreds restored the main play to favor, it was still without the Sly scenes. In this form it was continuously played —it was a magnificent vehicle for a man-and-woman star team, especially when the lady was getting just a little bit beyond Juliet and Ophelia. Of recent years Sly, too, has been restored to us—triumphantly by the Lunts, for instance, in 1935 and subsequent revivals. Nowadays Shrews are perpetually Tamed from the TV studios of New York to the festivals of Oregon, and we have been somewhat naïvely exhorted to "brush up our Shakespeare" by Cole Porter in *Kiss Me, Kate*.

There is an abiding vitality in this play; whatever its

merits or demerits, it is "box-office." It is always wisest, with Shakespeare, to start from the premise that he knew what he was up to, and not to begin scrambling his methods or distorting his conclusions until you are very sure that you know better. The problems and weaknesses will declare themselves soon enough. It is good to range yourself on the author's side and try to find out just why he did what he did. Then, if modern conditions, requirements, or responses seem to necessitate what I may call a "new translation" of the original, you will at least know what you are translating.

Yet, in the case of *The Taming of the Shrew,* there is little necessity for respectful orthodoxy. It is fair game for the high spirits of actors and director—provided the actors are likable (this is very important) and have the genuine comic gleam, and that the director is inventive, as an interpreter of the play and not just to demonstrate his own cleverness. For this is a farce; and farce, of all the forms of dramatic literature, is in the nature of a scenario, the raw material for its interpreters. It is a free-wheeling formula in which the author provides the comic situations and as many funny "gags" as he can think of and then relies on the age-old arts of vaudeville, the topical caricature, the personal trade-marks of the "clown," the stage business, the whole bag of tricks which cannot be put down in cold print. *The Shrew* needs all these; they must be beguiling to eye, ear, and heart, not forced or ugly. But within these limits I do not think Shakespeare would object to the wildest extravaganzas on his written theme—provided they do not betray its essence.

For in the playing of farce it is vital to remember one thing—the truth; the desperate importance of being in earnest. A caricature is not funny unless the original is recognizable behind the comic distortion. So the characters in farce must be an extension of reality: truth carried beyond accurate reproduction, carried with remorseless logic to the pitch of absurdity. It is one of the noteworthy strengths of *The Shrew* that it is full of good parts with "meat" in them. They are not made of cardboard, even the smallest of them, and it is the business of the actors to give them genuine purpose and life.

Baptista, for instance, is a very recognizable father. He is rich, conventional, and a widower, considerably exercised about the bringing up of two motherless girls, one of whom he takes (quite wrongly) to be the soul of sweet obedience, and the other, who frankly terrifies him to death. He cannot understand one thing about her. But he does try; and he tries quite desperately to be fair and equal in his dealings, with a ponderous and reluctant impartiality which has the effect of infuriating his elder "problem child" more than ever. These are the "bones" of Baptista, and though the part is not one of the showiest in the play, it is a sound one; the peripheral fuddy-duddy-ness, the backing and filling and comic mixture of fright and good-will are the farcical trimmings.

Similarly with Gremio, who is excellently observed and might stand for his own phrase of "an old Italian fox"— shrewd, self-made, no doubt somewhat overdressed and affected—betraying the blood of his Commedia dell' Arte prototype, Pantalone; but not without pathos, either (witness his rueful "my cake is dough" when Bianca marries Lucentio), and a very penetrating observer. His description of the "mad marriage" is one of the best things in the play. Hortensio is a fashionable young man, Princeton probably, who no doubt plays an excellent game of golf and is a great asset at a party. He hasn't a great deal of humor about himself and is especially determined not to be pushed around. "I will be married to a wealthy widow," he proudly asserts, refusing to pine for the faithless Bianca, and it is not without a tiny spark of satisfaction that we observe the meekness of his subsequent behavior.

There is plenty of character in Tranio too. We must not think of him as a "servant" in our modern meaning. He was probably of good family himself, brought up, as young men were in those days, attached to the noble house to which he was probably related or to whom his father had rendered service. He is more like a foster-brother to Lucentio than a valet. But there is nevertheless considerable fun to be had from his being just a little too genteel, just a little too ready with his tag-Latin, just a little too well-dressed for the occasion, retaining a faint whiff of the gentleman's gentleman. Lucentio is a trifle less sharp. He must have good looks and a good voice, though he has less poetry than most of Shakespeare's handsome juveniles. But he has enough humor to save him from being a stuffed shirt, and his behavior both to his servants and, at the end, to his father is straightforward and agreeable. Much may be forgiven to anyone so much in love.

Biondello is a rapid and lively sketch, full of speed and mischief, a little monkey of a fellow. It is permissible, I think, to embellish him with snatches of song and dance; also the actor must have plenty of breath and faultless enunciation to tackle the description of Petruchio's arrival for the wedding at the pace which it demands. Grumio is more significant stuff. The part must have been played by the "clown" of Shakespeare's company and it needs the clown's personality and invention. But behind this there is a solid core of loyalty and common sense. "Your ancient, trusty, pleasant servant, Grumio," says Hortensio to Petruchio, and to us, also, it should be unthinkable that they should ever part. Grumio may be excessively literal-minded, and is long accustomed to being the patsy of his master's escapades; but he has enough devotion for six.

Similarly with the other smaller parts. The Pedant is a dear little man, terribly willing and with no humor whatever. Tradition has it that in Act V, Scene 1, where he confronts Vincentio, he has been plied with rather too much wine. But this should not mean that he falls over his feet and cannot talk straight; rather, that he is more in earnest than ever and overplays his part out of sheer zeal. The Tailor is another tiny sketch executed with all the brilliance Shakespeare knew how to display within so small a compass—a dandified fellow, tremendously proud of his artistic creations and baffled to the point of frenzy by his apparently crazy clients. The opportunities for "funny business" in the Tailor scene are endless—and perfectly legitimate so long as he remembers who he is and what he has come for. So with the Petruchio servants. The scenes in which they appear are, of necessity, thick with every kind of visual "gag," many of them traditional and some, I have no doubt, going back to Shakespeare's own time. But they must never forget the basic intention of their endeavors—to provide the most magnificent possible welcome for their master and his blushing bride. It is this over-eagerness, this stumbling absurdity of haste, that lends point to the poor "rascal cook" who really has NOT burnt the mutton, to the boy who brings the water and gets it thrown all over him, to the wretched youth who pulls so hard at Petruchio's boots that he falls head over heels and capsizes the bride in his efforts. Above all, the actors must behave as if the entire situation were new to them and not one thing in it had ever happened before. Spontaneity and precision are the secrets of playing farce.

One word about Bianca, popularly supposed to be the "ingenue" of the piece, the sweetly pretty little thing, the model of decorum. She is, in fact, a little minx. She flirts shamelessly with whoever comes along, capitalizes on her father's devotion, darts catty little remarks at her sister whenever she dares, and covers all this with a smug, butter-wouldn't-melt-in-the-mouth demureness guaranteed to drive Kate absolutely mad.

This is important, for Kate leaps into the play seen only from the point of view of people who fear and dislike her. It is vital for the actress to decide why she is what she is. I see her as a "modern" woman, of intellect, courage, and enormous energy of mind and body, shut up in a society where women were supposed only to look decorative, do embroidery and play on the virginals and the lute. The point of being a young girl is to get married. And Kate doesn't particularly want to get married; she thinks the fashionable young men of Padua beneath contempt. She despises her father, who is so obviously afraid of her, and her silly, pretty, popular, horrid little sister is the very last straw. She takes exasperated refuge in terrifying everybody in sight. Except, of course, Petruchio.

These are two people full of flaming vitality and it is their story which is the core of the play and the reason for its enduring popularity. But the interpretation of this theme is by no means foolproof. If Katharine is played simply as "an irksome, brawling scold" and Petruchio as a "mad-brained rudesby, full of spleen"—a fortune-hunter at that —their story will indeed seem brutal. It will be nothing but the subjection of intolerable bad temper by equally intolerable physical violence. But there is more wit in it than that, and very much more humanity.

Suppose that the two of them do actually fall in love— he, certainly, when he first sets eyes on her; she, perhaps, when she finds herself, willy-nilly, in his arms. Neither, however, knows it of the other, nor will they admit it to themselves. This means that the wooing scene must be played with finesse, not just as a series of kicks and scuffles. But a few pauses, a few inflections will be enough. We know that these are two people of stature and that they are meant for each other.

The contest becomes, in part, a game of wits. We want it to be resolved and we know that Katharine, in her heart, wants it as much as we do. It is her pride that must be broken, not her spirit. Petruchio could never have endured a tame wife. Meanwhile, the antagonists deal blow and counterblow with a zest which is increasingly informed with love and is finally overwhelmed in laughter.

Katharine's final "surrender" is full of irony and wit. Agreeing, with deceptive docility, to call Vincentio "fair, lovely maid," and to accept the sun and moon as interchangeable planets, she contrives triumphantly to better Petruchio's instruction. "Pardon, old father, my mistaking eyes, That have been so bedazzled with the . . ."—here a pause and she shoots a glance at her husband—". . . sun?" And he nods delighted agreement.

She has not become a cipher; she has only changed her

technique. Her final speech, all honey and velvet, is full of a delicious realization that if women's lances are but straws, their weakness is indeed "past compare"; and that to "serve, love and obey" in all outward seeming is the surest road to victory. She and her Petruchio come together in a new wisdom and a beautifully negotiated peace.

There is one other character in the play of almost equal stature, Christopher Sly, "old Sly's son of Burton Heath, by birth a pedlar, by education a card-maker, by transmutation a bear-herd, and now by present profession a tinker." We know him well, the old rascal; he is of a vintage which "came in with Richard Conqueror," and he is a great addition to any "pleasant comedy." Moreover, his scenes embody the device of the strolling players, who are hired to play before him; and this, in turn, puts the whole "joke within a joke" into just the right perspective of extravagant make-believe.

It also gives the modern director exactly the freedom he needs. For the Players and their Host can be of any period —they can wear anything, sing anything, do—almost— anything. I once made them Victorian, much like Vincent Crummles and his famous troupe in *Nicholas Nickleby*. They are a "fit-up" company, ready to turn their hands to anything. Their idea of "dressing the part"—like Shakespeare's own actors, too—is to add a few ostentatious "period" items to their own clothes, an eclectic assortment of "ruffs and cuffs and farthingales and things," "scarfs and fans and double change of bravery."

They scatter the proceedings with songs and dances, equally to their own choice. Mine included some Victorian balladry—a solemn greeting to Petruchio and his bride, for instance, beginning "Hail, wedded bliss"—and some irreverent musical quotations from the Wedding March and the Overture to William Tell. The action, too, takes from the strolling players the same freedom as their costumes and music. They bring their own props with them (a curious assortment) and since the whole performance takes place in the Hall of the Lord's House, they arrange its existing features and facilities as they go along. These, obviously, can include some perfectly splendid scenery borrowed from the local community theater, or no extraneous scenery at all—which will give you something very like an Elizabethan stage. I do not think this is too free a counsel, for what to the players—or to Shakespeare—are the realistic niceties of the true Padua? And who cares at what period of History a Shrew is Tamed, provided she lives happily ever after?

But the use of the Induction scenes raises one considerable problem: it introduces us to Sly, spends two scenes on him, and then drops him completely after the four speeches which follow Act I, Scene 1. Probably the actor was needed to double in another part; in any case Shakespeare had other spectators seated on his platform stage and Sly's presence or absence was not so unusual and obtrusive as it is for us.

My own advice to the director is to raid the rest of the Sly material which is to be found in the other *"Shrew"* play, *The Taming of a Shrew*. Whether this piece was the source-material for Shakespeare or whether it is a garbled derivative from him, it is certainly a close relation; and it contains two "inserts" for Sly and Co., one after Act I, Scene 2, and one during Act V, Scene 1, where Sly protests furiously: "We'll have no sending to prison, that's flat." There is also what we would call a "pay-off" for Sly at the end, or at least the suggestion of one, which can be built into a final song-and-dance curtain of general "mirth and merriment"—or, for that matter, can send a chastened Sly rather sadly home, lamenting his lost dream.

In my own production, I kept Sly on-stage until the Intermission which followed Act III, Scene 2. (This scene, incidentally, is almost invariably cut at the exit of Petruchio and Katharine, which is the obvious "curtain.") Since, in the following scenes, everybody is much too busy to bother with him, I quite arbitrarily "lost" him, till he came galloping back—presumably from a drunken sleep—in the wake of the Petruchio-Vincentio party on its way to Padua (End of Act IV, Scene 5). He then remained till the end of the play and I used the tiny Epilogue from *A Shrew*.

For the rest, I never felt it necessary to alter the text very much, apart from minor line-cutting. I did curtail the intricacies of the sub-plot in the second half, telescoping Act IV, Scene 2 and Scene 4 in order to make one scene of them and keep the Petruchio story in continuous movement. Hazlitt's "animation and rapidity of action" are crucial to this play. For the rest, let the actors attack it with gaiety of soul and a high heart; then Sly may with confidence turn to his friends, the audience, and say: "Come, sit by my side and let the world slip: we shall ne'er be younger."

DRAMATIS PERSONAE

A LORD.
CHRISTOPHER SLY, *a tinker.*
HOSTESS, PAGE, PLAYERS,
   HUNTSMEN, *and* SERVANTS.
} Persons in the Induction.

BAPTISTA MINOLA, *a gentleman of Padua.*
VINCENTIO, *a merchant of Pisa.*
LUCENTIO, *son to Vincentio, in love with Bianca.*
PETRUCHIO, *a gentleman of Verona, a suitor to Katharine.*
GREMIO,
HORTENSIO,
} *suitors to Bianca.*

TRANIO,
BIONDELLO,
} *servants to Lucentio.*

GRUMIO,
CURTIS,
} *servants to Petruchio.*
A PEDANT.
KATHARINE,
BIANCA,
} *daughters to Baptista.*
A WIDOW.
TAILOR, HABERDASHER, *and* SERVANTS.

SCENE: *Padua, and Petruchio's house in the country.*

The Taming of the Shrew

Induction Scene one

> *Before an alehouse on a heath. Enter*
> *Hostess and Sly.*

SLY

I'll pheeze you in faith.

HOSTESS

A pair of stocks you rogue!

SLY

Y'are a baggage, the Slys are no rogues. Look in
the Chronicles, we came in with Richard Conqueror. Therefore paucas pallabris, let the world   5
slide. Sessa!

HOSTESS

You will not pay for the glasses you have burst?

SLY

No, not a denier. Go by Saint Jeronimy, go to
thy cold bed, and warm thee.   10

HOSTESS

I know my remedy; I must go fetch the third-
borough.   [*Exit*.

A complete Glossary of Elizabethan terms begins
on page 187.

SLY

Third, or fourth, or fifth borough, I'll answer
him by law. I'll not budge an inch boy. Let him
come, and kindly.   15

> [*Lies down on the ground and falls asleep.*
> *Horns winded. Enter Lord from hunting,*
> *with Huntsmen and Servants.*

LORD

Huntsman I charge thee, tender well my hounds.
Breathe Merriman, the poor cur is embossed,
And couple Clowder with the deep-mouthed
    brach.
Saw'st thou not boy how Silver made it good
At the hedge-corner, in the coldest fault?   20
I would not lose the dog for twenty pound.

FIRST HUNTSMAN

Why Belman is as good as he my lord.
He cried upon it at the merest loss,
And twice to-day picked out the dullest scent,
Trust me, I take him for the better dog.   25

LORD

Thou art a fool. If Echo were as fleet,
I would esteem him worth a dozen such.
But sup them well, and look unto them all.
To-morrow I intend to hunt again.

FIRST HUNTSMAN

I will my lord.   30

LORD

What's here? One dead, or drunk? See, doth he
    breathe?

SECOND HUNTSMAN

He breathes my lord. Were he not warmed with
    ale,
This were a bed but cold to sleep so soundly.

LORD

O monstrous beast, how like a swine he lies.
Grim death, how foul and loathsome is thine
    image.   35
Sirs, I will practise on this drunken man.
What think you, if he were conveyed to bed,
Wrapped in sweet clothes, rings put upon his fin-
    gers,
A most delicious banquet by his bed,
And brave attendants near him when he wakes,   40
Would not the beggar then forget himself?

FIRST HUNTSMAN

Believe me lord, I think he cannot choose.

SECOND HUNTSMAN

It would seem strange unto him when he waked.

LORD

Even as a flattering dream, or worthless fancy.
Then take him up, and manage well the jest.   45
Carry him gently to my fairest chamber,
And hang it round with all my wanton pictures.
Balm his foul head in warm distilled waters,
And burn sweet wood to make the lodging sweet.
Procure me music ready when he wakes,   50
To make a dulcet and a heavenly sound;
And if he chance to speak, be ready straight
And with a low submissive reverence

Say, what is it your honour will command?
Let one attend him with a silver basin   55
Full of rose-water, and bestrewed with flowers;
Another bear the ewer, the third a diaper,
And say, will't please your lordship cool your
    hands?
Some one be ready with a costly suit,
And ask him what apparel he will wear.   60
Another tell him of his hounds and horse,
And that his lady mourns at his disease.
Persuade him that he hath been lunatic;
And when he says he is Sly, say that he dreams,
For he is nothing but a mighty lord.   65
This do, and do it kindly, gentle sirs,
It will be pastime passing excellent,
If it be husbanded with modesty.

   FIRST HUNTSMAN

My lord, I warrant you we'll play our part,
As he shall think by our true diligence   70
He is no less than what we say he is.

   LORD

Take him up gently, and to bed with him,
And each one to his office when he wakes.
     [*Sly is borne out. Trumpets sound.*
Sirrah, go see what trumpet 'tis that sounds.
       [*Exit Servant.*
Belike some noble gentleman that means,   75
Travelling some journey, to repose him here.
   Enter Servant.
How now? Who is it?

SERVANT

           An it please your honour,
Players that offer service to your lordship.

LORD

Bid them come near.

     Enter Players.

            Now fellows, you are welcome.

PLAYERS

We thank your honour.   80

LORD

Do you intend to stay with me to-night?

FIRST PLAYER

So please your lordship to accept our duty.

LORD

With all my heart. This fellow I remember,
Since once he played a farmer's eldest son.
'Twas where you wooed the gentlewoman so
    well.   85
I have forgot your name; but sure that part
Was aptly fitted, and naturally performed.

FIRST PLAYER

I think 'twas Soto that your honour means.

LORD

'Tis very true, thou didst it excellent.
Well you are come to me in happy time,   90
The rather for I have some sport in hand,
Wherein your cunning can assist me much.
There is a lord will hear you play to-night;
But I am doubtful of your modesties,
Lest over-eyeing of his odd behaviour—   95

For yet his honour never heard a play—
You break into some merry passion,
And so offend him; for I tell you sirs,
If you should smile, he grows impatient.

FIRST PLAYER

Fear not my lord, we can contain ourselves,   100
Were he the veriest antic in the world.

LORD

Go sirrah, take them to the buttery,
And give them friendly welcome every one.
Let them want nothing that my house affords.

                    [*Exit Servant with the Players.*

[*To another Servant.*] Sirrah go you to
    Barthol'mew my page,   105
And see him dressed in all suits like a lady.
That done, conduct him to the drunkard's
    chamber,
And call him madam, do him obeisance.
Tell him from me, as he will win my love,
He bear himself with honourable action,   110
Such as he hath observed in noble ladies
Unto their lords, by them accomplished;
Such duty to the drunkard let him do,
With soft low tongue and lowly courtesy,
And say, what is't your honour will command,   115
Wherein your lady, and your humble wife,
May show her duty, and make known her love?
And then with kind embracements, tempting
    kisses,
And with declining head into his bosom,

Bid him shed tears, as being overjoyed   120
To see her noble lord restored to health,
Who for twice seven years hath esteemed him
No better than a poor and loathsome beggar.
And if the boy have not a woman's gift
To rain a shower of commanded tears,   125
An onion will do well for such a shift,
Which in a napkin being close conveyed,
Shall in despite enforce a watery eye.
See this dispatched with all the haste thou canst,
Anon I'll give thee more instructions.   130

                             [Exit Servant.

I know the boy will well usurp the grace,
Voice, gait, and action of a gentlewoman.
I long to hear him call the drunkard husband,
And how my men will stay themselves from
    laughter,
When they do homage to this simple peasant.   135
I'll in to counsel them; haply my presence
May well abate the over-merry spleen,
Which otherwise would grow into extremes.

                              [Exeunt.

Scene two

*A bedchamber in the Lord's house. Sly
discovered, with Attendants; some with
apparel, basin, ewer, and other appur-
tenances; and Lord.*

SLY

For God's sake a pot of small ale.

FIRST SERVANT

Will't please your lordship drink a cup of sack?

SECOND SERVANT

Will't please your honour taste of these conserves?

THIRD SERVANT

What raiment will your honour wear to-day?

SLY

I am Christophero Sly, call not me honour nor   5
lordship. I ne'er drank sack in my life. And if
you give me any conserves, give me conserves of
beef. Ne'er ask me what raiment I'll wear, for I
have no more doublets than backs, no more
stockings than legs, nor no more shoes than feet,   10
nay sometime more feet than shoes, or such
shoes as my toes look through the overleather.

LORD

Heaven cease this idle humour in your honour.
O that a mighty man of such descent,   15
Of such possessions, and so high esteem,
Should be infused with so foul a spirit!

SLY

What would you make me mad? Am not I Christopher Sly, old Sly's son of Burton-heath, by
birth a pedlar, by education a card-maker, by   20
transmutation a bear-herd, and now by present
profession a tinker? Ask Marian Hacket the fat
ale-wife of Wincot, if she know me not. If she say
I am not fourteen pence on the score for sheer
ale, score me up for the lying'st knave in Chris-   25
tendom. What, I am not bestraught; here's—

FIRST SERVANT

O this it is that makes your lady mourn.

SECOND SERVANT

O this it is that makes your servants droop.

LORD

Hence comes it, that your kindred shuns your
    house,   30
As beaten hence by your strange lunacy.
O noble lord, bethink thee of thy birth,
Call home thy ancient thoughts from banish-
    ment,
And banish hence these abject lowly dreams.
Look how thy servants do attend on thee,   35
Each in his office ready at thy beck.
Wilt thou have music? Hark, Apollo plays,
                                        [*Music*.
And twenty caged nightingales do sing.
Or wilt thou sleep? We'll have thee to a couch
Softer and sweeter than the lustful bed   40
On purpose trimmed up for Semiramis.

Say thou wilt walk; we will bestrew the ground.
Or wilt thou ride? Thy horses shall be trapped,
Their harness studded all with gold and pearl.
Dost thou love hawking? Thou hast hawks will
    soar   45
Above the morning lark. Or wilt thou hunt,
Thy hounds shall make the welkin answer them,
And fetch shrill echoes from the hollow earth.

   FIRST SERVANT

Say thou wilt course, thy greyhounds are as swift
As breathed stags, ay, fleeter than the roe.   50

   SECOND SERVANT

Dost thou love pictures? We will fetch thee
    straight
Adonis painted by a running brook,
And Cytherea all in sedges hid,
Which seem to move and wanton with her
    breath,
Even as the waving sedges play with wind.   55

   LORD

We'll show thee Io, as she was a maid,
And how she was beguiled and surprised,
As lively painted as the deed was done.

   THIRD SERVANT

Or Daphne roaming through a thorny wood,
Scratching her legs, that one shall swear she
    bleeds,   60
And at that sight shall sad Apollo weep,
So workmanly the blood and tears are drawn.

LORD

Thou art a lord, and nothing but a lord.
Thou hast a lady far more beautiful,
Than any woman in this waning age.   65

FIRST SERVANT

And till the tears that she hath shed for thee
Like envious floods o'er-run her lovely face.
She was the fairest creature in the world,
And yet she is inferior to none.

SLY

Am I a lord, and have I such a lady?   70
Or do I dream? Or have I dreamed till now?
I do not sleep. I see, I hear, I speak.
I smell sweet savours, and I feel soft things.
Upon my life I am a lord indeed,
And not a tinker, nor Christopher Sly.   75
Well, bring our lady hither to our sight,
And once again a pot o' th' smallest ale.

SECOND SERVANT

Will't please your mightiness to wash your
    hands?
        [*Servants present basin, &c.*
O how we joy to see your wit restored!
O that once more you knew but what you are!   80
These fifteen years you have been in a dream,
Or when you waked, so waked as if you slept.

SLY

These fifteen years! By my fay, a goodly nap.
But did I never speak of all that time?

FIRST SERVANT

O yes my lord, but very idle words,   85
For though you lay here in this goodly chamber,
Yet would you say, ye were beaten out of door,
And rail upon the hostess of the house,
And say you would present her at the leet,
Because she brought stone jugs, and no sealed
    quarts.   90
Sometimes you would call out for Cicely Hacket.

SLY

Ay, the woman's maid of the house.

THIRD SERVANT

Why sir you know no house, nor no such maid,
Nor no such men as you have reckoned up,
As Stephen Sly, and old John Naps of Greece,   95
And Peter Turph, and Henry Pimpernell,
And twenty more such names and men as these,
Which never were, nor no man ever saw.

SLY

Now Lord be thanked for my good amends.

ALL

Amen.   100

SLY

I thank thee: thou shalt not lose by it.
        Enter Page as a lady, with Attendants.

PAGE

How fares my noble lord?

SLY

Marry I fare well, for here is cheer enough.
Where is my wife?

PAGE

Here noble lord, what is thy will with her?   105

SLY

Are you my wife, and will not call me husband?
My men should call me lord, I am your good-
man.

PAGE

My husband and my lord, my lord and husband.
I am your wife in all obedience.

SLY

I know it well. What must I call her?   110

LORD

Madam.

SLY

Al'ce madam, or Joan madam?

LORD

Madam, and nothing else, so lords call ladies.

SLY

Madam wife, they say that I have dreamed,
And slept above some fifteen year or more.   115

PAGE

Ay, and the time seems thirty unto me,
Being all this time abandoned from your bed.

SLY

'Tis much. Servants, leave me and her alone.
Madam undress you, and come now to bed.

PAGE

Thrice-noble lord, let me entreat of you   120
To pardon me yet for a night or two.
Or if not so, until the sun be set.

For your physicians have expressly charged,
In peril to incur your former malady,
That I should yet absent me from your bed.   125
I hope this reason stands for my excuse.

SLY

Ay, it stands so that I may hardly tarry so long.
But I would be loth to fall into my dreams again.
I will therefore tarry in despite of the flesh and
the blood.   130

Enter Messenger.

MESSENGER

Your honour's players, hearing your amendment,
Are come to play a pleasant comedy.
For so your doctors hold it very meet,
Seeing too much sadness hath congealed your
    blood,
And melancholy is the nurse of frenzy;   135
Therefore they thought it good you hear a play,
And frame your mind to mirth and merriment,
Which bars a thousand harms, and lengthens life.

SLY

Marry I will, let them play it. Is not a comonty a   140
Christmas gambol, or a tumbling-trick?

PAGE

No my good lord, it is more pleasing stuff.

SLY

What, household stuff?

PAGE

It is a kind of history.

SLY

Well, we'll see't. Come madam wife sit by my 145
side, and let the world slip, we shall ne'er be
younger.   [*Flourish.*

Act one Scene one

   Padua. A Square.
   Enter Lucentio and Tranio.

LUCENTIO

Tranio, since for the great desire I had
To see fair Padua, nursery of arts,
I am arrived for fruitful Lombardy,
The pleasant garden of great Italy,
And by my father's love and leave am armed   5
With his good will, and thy good company,
My trusty servant, well approved in all,
Here let us breathe, and haply institute
A course of learning, and ingenious studies.
Pisa renowned for grave citizens   10
Gave me my being and my father first,
A merchant of great traffic through the world,
Vincentio, come of the Bentivolii.
Vincentio's son, brought up in Florence,
It shall become to serve all hopes conceived   15
To deck his fortune with his virtuous deeds.
And therefore Tranio, for the time I study
Virtue, and that part of philosophy
Will I apply that treats of happiness
By virtue specially to be achieved.   20
Tell me thy mind, for I have Pisa left,

And am to Padua come, as he that leaves
A shallow plash, to plunge him in the deep,
And with satiety seeks to quench his thirst.

TRANIO

Mi perdonato, gentle master mine.   25
I am in all affected as yourself,
Glad that you thus continue your resolve
To suck the sweets of sweet philosophy.
Only, good master, while we do admire
This virtue, and this moral discipline,   30
Let's be no stoics, nor no stocks, I pray,
Or so devote to Aristotle's checks,
As Ovid be an outcast quite abjured.
Balk logic with acquaintance that you have,
And practise rhetoric in your common talk;   35
Music and poesy use, to quicken you;
The mathematics, and the metaphysics,
Fall to them, as you find your stomach serves
    you.
No profit grows, where is no pleasure ta'en.
In brief sir, study what you most affect.   40

LUCENTIO

Gramercies Tranio, well dost thou advise.
If Biondello thou wert come ashore,
We could at once put us in readiness,
And take a lodging fit to entertain
Such friends as time in Padua shall beget.   45

   Enter Baptista with Katharine and Bi-
   anca, Gremio, and Hortensio. Lucentio
   and Tranio stand aside.

But stay awhile, what company is this?
> TRANIO

Master, some show to welcome us to town.
> BAPTISTA

Gentlemen, importune me no further,
For how I firmly am resolved you know.
That is, not to bestow my youngest daughter,   50
Before I have a husband for the elder.
If either of you both love Katharina,
Because I know you well, and love you well,
Leave shall you have to court her at your
    pleasure.
> GREMIO

To cart her rather. She's too rough for me.   55
There, there, Hortensio, will you any wife?
> KATHARINE [*to Baptista*]

I pray you sir, is it your will
To make a stale of me amongst these mates?
> HORTENSIO

Mates, maid, how mean you that? No mates for
    you,
Unless you were of gentler, milder mould.   60
> KATHARINE

I' faith sir, you shall never need to fear.
Iwis it is not half way to her heart.
But if it were, doubt not, her care should be
To comb your noddle with a three-legged stool,
And paint your face, and use you like a fool.   65
> HORTENSIO

From all such devils, good Lord deliver us.

GREMIO

And me too, good Lord.

TRANIO [*aside to Lucentio*]

Hush master, here's some good pastime toward.
That wench is stark mad, or wonderful froward.

LUCENTIO [*aside to Tranio*]

But in the other's silence do I see   70
Maid's mild behaviour and sobriety.
Peace Tranio.

TRANIO [*aside to Lucentio*]

Well said master, mum! And gaze your fill.

BAPTISTA

Gentlemen, that I may soon make good
What I have said, Bianca get you in,   75
And let it not displease thee good Bianca,
For I will love thee ne'er the less my girl.

KATHARINE

A pretty peat, it is best put finger in the eye, an
she knew why.

BIANCA

Sister content you, in my discontent.   80
Sir, to your pleasure humbly I subscribe.
My books and instruments shall be my company,
On them to look, and practise by myself.

LUCENTIO [*aside to Tranio*]

Hark Tranio, thou mayst hear Minerva speak.

HORTENSIO

Signior Baptista, will you be so strange?   85
Sorry am I that our good will effects
Bianca's grief.

GREMIO

        Why will you mew her up,
Signior Baptista, for this fiend of hell,
And make her bear the penance of her tongue?

BAPTISTA

Gentlemen content ye. I am resolved. 90
Go in Bianca.   [*Exit Bianca.*
And for I know she taketh most delight
In music, instruments, and poetry,
Schoolmasters will I keep within my house,
Fit to instruct her youth. If you Hortensio, 95
Or Signior Gremio, you know any such,
Prefer them hither; for to cunning men
I will be very kind, and liberal
To mine own children in good bringing-up.
And so farewell. Katharina you may stay, 100
For I have more to commune with Bianca. [*Exit.*

KATHARINE

Why, and I trust I may go too, may I not? What,
shall I be appointed hours, as though belike, I
knew not what to take, and what to leave, ha? 105
                       [*Exit.*

GREMIO

You may go to the devil's dam. Your gifts are so
good here's none will hold you there. Love is not
so great Hortensio, but we may blow our nails
together, and fast it fairly out. Our cake's dough
on both sides. Farewell; yet for the love I bear 110
my sweet Bianca, if I can by any means light on

a fit man to teach her that wherein she delights, I
will wish him to her father.

HORTENSIO

So will I Signior Gremio. But a word I pray. 115
Though the nature of our quarrel yet never
brooked parle, know now upon advice, it touch-
eth us both—that we may yet again have access
to our fair mistress, and be happy rivals in Bianca's love—to labour and effect one thing specially. 120

GREMIO

What's that I pray?

HORTENSIO

Marry sir to get a husband for her sister.

GREMIO

A husband? A devil. 125

HORTENSIO

I say a husband.

GREMIO

I say, a devil. Think'st thou Hortensio, though
her father be very rich, any man is so very a fool
to be married to hell?

HORTENSIO

Tush Gremio. Though it pass your patience and 130
mine to endure her loud alarums, why man, there
be good fellows in the world, an a man could
light on them, would take her with all faults, and
money enough.

GREMIO

I cannot tell; but I had as lief take her dowry 135

with this condition——to be whipped at the high-
cross every morning.

    HORTENSIO

Faith, as you say, there's small choice in rotten
apples. But come, since this bar in law makes us
friends, it shall be so far forth friendly main-   140
tained, till by helping Baptista's eldest daughter
to a husband, we set his youngest free for a husband, and then have to't afresh. Sweet Bianca!
Happy man be his dole. He that runs fastest, gets   145
the ring. How say you Signior Gremio?

    GREMIO

I am agreed, and would I had given him the best
horse in Padua to begin his wooing that would
thoroughly woo her, wed her, and bed her, and
rid the house of her. Come on.   150

            [*Exeunt Gremio and Hortensio.*

    TRANIO

I pray sir tell me, is it possible
That love should of a sudden take such hold?

    LUCENTIO

O Tranio, till I found it to be true,
I never thought it possible or likely.
But see, while idly I stood looking on,   155
I found the effect of love in idleness,
And now in plainness do confess to thee,
That art to me as secret and as dear
As Anna to the Queen of Carthage was——
Tranio I burn, I pine, I perish Tranio,   160
If I achieve not this young modest girl.

Counsel me Tranio, for I know thou canst.
Assist me Tranio, for I know thou wilt.

TRANIO

Master, it is no time to chide you now;
Affection is not rated from the heart. 165
If love have touched you, naught remains but so,
Redime te captum quam queas minimo.

LUCENTIO

Gramercies lad. Go forward, this contents.
The rest will comfort, for thy counsel's sound.

TRANIO

Master, you looked so longly on the maid, 170
Perhaps you marked not what's the pith of all.

LUCENTIO

O yes, I saw sweet beauty in her face,
Such as the daughter of Agenor had,
That made great Jove to humble him to her
hand,
When with his knees he kissed the Cretan
strand. 175

TRANIO

Saw you no more? Marked you not how her
sister
Began to scold, and raise up such a storm,
That mortal ears might hardly endure the din?

LUCENTIO

Tranio, I saw her coral lips to move,
And with her breath she did perfume the air. 180
Sacred and sweet was all I saw in her.

TRANIO

Nay, then 'tis time to stir him from his trance.

I pray awake sir. If you love the maid,

Bend thoughts and wits to achieve her. Thus it
   stands.

Her elder sister is so curst and shrewd,   185

That till the father rid his hands of her,

Master, your love must live a maid at home,

And therefore has he closely mewed her up,

Because she will not be annoyed with suitors.

LUCENTIO

Ah Tranio, what a cruel father's he.   190

But art thou not advised, he took some care

To get her cunning schoolmasters to instruct
   her?

TRANIO

Ay marry am I sir, and now 'tis plotted.

LUCENTIO

I have it Tranio.

TRANIO

                Master, for my hand,

Both our inventions meet and jump in one.   195

LUCENTIO

Tell me thine first.

TRANIO

                You will be schoolmaster,

And undertake the teaching of the maid.

That's your device.

LUCENTIO

            It is. May it be done?

TRANIO

Not possible; for who shall bear your part,
And be in Padua here Vincentio's son,   200
Keep house, and ply his book, welcome his
    friends,
Visit his countrymen, and banquet them?

LUCENTIO

Basta, content thee, for I have it full.
We have not yet been seen in any house,
Nor can we be distinguished by our faces,   205
For man or master. Then it follows thus—
Thou shalt be master, Tranio, in my stead,
Keep house, and port, and servants, as I should.
I will some other be, some Florentine,
Some Neapolitan, or meaner man of Pisa.   210
'Tis hatched, and shall be so. Tranio, at once
Uncase thee; take my coloured hat and cloak.
When Biondello comes, he waits on thee,
But I will charm him first to keep his tongue.

TRANIO

So had you need.   [*They exchange habits.*   215
In brief sir, sith it your pleasure is,
And I am tied to be obedient—
For so your father charged me at our parting,
Be serviceable to my son, quoth he,
Although I think 'twas in another sense—   220
I am content to be Lucentio,
Because so well I love Lucentio.

LUCENTIO

Tranio be so, because Lucentio loves,

And let me be a slave, t' achieve that maid,
Whose sudden sight hath thralled my wounded
  eye.   225

     Enter Biondello.

Here comes the rogue. Sirrah, where have you
  been?

    BIONDELLO

Where have I been? Nay how now, where are
you? Master, has my fellow Tranio stolen your
clothes, or you stolen his, or both? Pray what's   230
the news?

    LUCENTIO

Sirrah come hither, 'tis no time to jest,
And therefore frame your manners to the time.
Your fellow Tranio here, to save my life,
Puts my apparel and my countenance on,
And I for my escape have put on his.   235
For in a quarrel since I came ashore,
I killed a man, and fear I was descried.
Wait you on him, I charge you, as becomes,
While I make way from hence to save my life.
You understand me?

    BIONDELLO
                I sir? Ne'er a whit.   240

    LUCENTIO

And not a jot of Tranio in your mouth.
Tranio is changed into Lucentio.

    BIONDELLO

The better for him, would I were so too.

TRANIO

So could I faith boy, to have the next wish after,
That Lucentio indeed had Baptista's youngest
    daughter.   245
But sirrah, not for my sake, but your master's,
    I advise
You use your manners discreetly in all kind of
    companies.
When I am alone, why then I am Tranio,
But in all places else, your master Lucentio.

LUCENTIO

Tranio let's go.
One thing more rests, that thyself execute,   250
To make one among these wooers. If thou ask
    me why,
Sufficeth, my reasons are both good and weighty.
                                        [*Exeunt.*

The Presenters above speak.

FIRST SERVANT

My lord you nod, you do not mind the play.

SLY

Yes by Saint Anne do I. A good matter surely.   255
Comes there any more of it?

PAGE

My lord 'tis but begun.

SLY

'Tis a very excellent piece of work, madam lady.
Would 'twere done.

Scene two

The same. Before Hortensio's house.
Enter Petruchio and Grumio.

PETRUCHIO

Verona, for awhile I take my leave,
To see my friends in Padua; but of all
My best beloved and approved friend
Hortensio; and I trow this is his house.
Here sirrah Grumio, knock I say.   5

GRUMIO

Knock sir? Whom should I knock? Is there any
man has rebused your worship?

PETRUCHIO

Villain, I say, knock me here soundly.

GRUMIO

Knock you here sir? Why sir, what am I sir, that
I should knock you here sir?   10

PETRUCHIO

Villain I say, knock me at this gate,
And rap me well, or I'll knock your knave's pate.

GRUMIO

My master is grown quarrelsome. I should
    knock you first,
And then I know after who comes by the worst.

PETRUCHIO

Will it not be?   15
Faith sirrah, an you'll not knock, I'll ring it,

I'll try how you can sol, fa, and sing it.
                    [*Wrings him by the ears.*

GRUMIO

Help masters help! My master is mad.

PETRUCHIO

Now knock when I bid you, sirrah villain.
        Enter Hortensio.

HORTENSIO

How now, what's the matter? My old friend   20
Grumio, and my good friend Petruchio! How
do you all at Verona?

PETRUCHIO

Signior Hortensio, come you to part the fray?
Con tutto il cuore ben trovato, may I say.

HORTENSIO

Alla nostra casa ben venuto, molto honorato   25
signior mio Petruchio.
Rise Grumio rise, we will compound this quarrel.

GRUMIO [*rising*]

Nay 'tis no matter sir, what he 'leges in Latin.
If this be not a lawful cause for me to leave his
service, look you sir. He bid me knock him, and   30
rap him soundly sir. Well, was it fit for a servant
to use his master so, being perhaps, for aught I
see, two and thirty, a pip out?
Whom would to God I had well knocked at first,
Then had not Grumio come by the worst.   35

PETRUCHIO

A senseless villain. Good Hortensio,
I bade the rascal knock upon your gate,

And could not get him for my heart to do it.
> GRUMIO

Knock at the gate? O heavens! Spake you not
these words plain, sirrah, knock me here; rap   40
me here; knock me well; and knock me soundly?
And come you now with knocking at the gate?
> PETRUCHIO

Sirrah be gone, or talk not, I advise you.
> HORTENSIO

Petruchio patience, I am Grumio's pledge.   45
Why this' a heavy chance 'twixt him and you,
Your ancient, trusty, pleasant servant Grumio.
And tell me now, sweet friend, what happy
    gale
Blows you to Padua here, from old Verona?
> PETRUCHIO

Such wind as scatters young men through the
    world,   50
To seek their fortunes further than at home,
Where small experience grows. But in a few,
Signior Hortensio, thus it stands with me.
Antonio my father is deceased,
And I have thrust myself into this maze,   55
Haply to wive and thrive, as best I may.
Crowns in my purse I have, and goods at home,
And so am come abroad to see the world.
> HORTENSIO

Petruchio, shall I then come roundly to thee,
And wish thee to a shrewd ill-favoured wife?   60
Thou'dst thank me but a little for my counsel.

And yet I'll promise thee she shall be rich,
And very rich. But thou'rt too much my friend,
And I'll not wish thee to her.

PETRUCHIO

Signior Hortensio, 'twixt such friends as we, 65
Few words suffice; and therefore, if thou know
One rich enough to be Petruchio's wife—
As wealth is burthen of my wooing dance—
Be she as foul as was Florentius' love,
As old as Sibyl, and as curst and shrewd 70
As Socrates' Xanthippe, or a worse,
She moves me not, or not removes at least
Affection's edge in me, were she as rough
As are the swelling Adriatic seas.
I come to wive it wealthily in Padua; 75
If wealthily, then happily in Padua.

GRUMIO

Nay look you sir, he tells you flatly what his
mind is. Why give him gold enough, and marry
him to a puppet or an aglet-baby; or an old trot
with ne'er a tooth in her head, though she have 80
as many diseases as two and fifty horses. Why
nothing comes amiss, so money comes withal.

HORTENSIO

Petruchio, since we are stepped thus far in,
I will continue that I broached in jest.
I can Petruchio help thee to a wife 85
With wealth enough, and young and beauteous,
Brought up as best becomes a gentlewoman.
Her only fault, and that is faults enough,

Is, that she is intolerable curst,
And shrewd, and froward, so beyond all meas-
ure,   90
That, were my state far worser than it is,
I would not wed her for a mine of gold.

    PETRUCHIO

Hortensio peace. Thou know'st not gold's effect.
Tell me her father's name, and 'tis enough.
For I will board her, though she chide as loud   95
As thunder, when the clouds in autumn crack.

    HORTENSIO

Her father is Baptista Minola,
An affable and courteous gentleman.
Her name is Katharina Minola,
Renowned in Padua for her scolding tongue.   100

    PETRUCHIO

I know her father, though I know not her,
And he knew my deceased father well.
I will not sleep Hortensio till I see her,
And therefore let me be thus bold with you,
To give you over at this first encounter,   105
Unless you will accompany me thither.

    GRUMIO

I pray you sir let him go while the humour lasts.
O' my word, an she knew him as well as I do, she
would think scolding would do little good upon
him. She may perhaps call him half a score   110
knaves, or so. Why that's nothing; an he begin
once, he'll rail in his rhetricks. I'll tell you what
sir, an she stand him but a little, he will throw a

figure in her face, and so disfigure her with it,
that she shall have no more eyes to see withal   115
than a cat. You know him not sir.

HORTENSIO

Tarry Petruchio, I must go with thee,
For in Baptista's keep my treasure is.
He hath the jewel of my life in hold,
His youngest daughter, beautiful Bianca,   120
And her withholds from me and other more,
Suitors to her and rivals in my love,
Supposing it a thing impossible,
For those defects I have before rehearsed,
That ever Katharina will be wooed.   125
Therefore this order hath Baptista ta'en,
That none shall have access unto Bianca,
Till Katharine the curst have got a husband.

GRUMIO

Katharine the curst,
A title for a maid, of all titles the worst.   130

HORTENSIO

Now shall my friend Petruchio do me grace,
And offer me, disguised in sober robes,
To old Baptista as a schoolmaster
Well seen in music, to instruct Bianca;
That so I may by this device at least   135
Have leave and leisure to make love to her,
And unsuspected court her by herself.

GRUMIO

Here's no knavery! See, to beguile the old folks,
how the young folks lay their heads together.   140

*Enter Gremio, and Lucentio disguised as
Cambio, a schoolmaster.*

Master, master, look about you. Who goes there,
ha?

HORTENSIO

Peace Grumio, it is the rival of my love.
Petruchio stand by awhile.

GRUMIO

A proper stripling and an amorous.

[*They stand aside.*

GREMIO

O very well; I have perused the note.   145
Hark you sir. I'll have them very fairly bound—
All books of love, see that at any hand—
And see you read no other lectures to her.
You understand me. Over and beside
Signior Baptista's liberality,   150
I'll mend it with a largess. Take your paper too,
And let me have them very well perfumed;
For she is sweeter than perfume itself,
To whom they go to. What will you read to her?

LUCENTIO

Whate'er I read to her, I'll plead for you,   155
As for my patron, stand you so assured,
As firmly as yourself were still in place;
Yea and perhaps with more successful words
Than you—unless you were a scholar sir.

GREMIO

O this learning, what a thing it is!   160

GRUMIO [*aside*]

O this woodcock, what an ass it is!

PETRUCHIO [*aside*]

Peace sirrah.

HORTENSIO

Grumio mum! [*Comes forward.*] God save you
  Signior Gremio.

GREMIO

And you are well met, Signior Hortensio.

Trow you whither I am going? To Baptista
  Minola.   165

I promised to enquire carefully

About a schoolmaster for the fair Bianca,

And by good fortune I have lighted well

On this young man; for learning and behaviour

Fit for her turn, well read in poetry   170

And other books, good ones, I warrant ye.

HORTENSIO

'Tis well; and I have met a gentleman

Hath promised me to help me to another,

A fine musician to instruct our mistress;

So shall I no whit be behind in duty   175

To fair Bianca, so beloved of me.

GREMIO

Beloved of me, and that my deeds shall prove.

GRUMIO [*aside*]

And that his bags shall prove.

HORTENSIO

Gremio, 'tis now no time to vent our love.

Listen to me, and if you speak me fair,   180

I'll tell you news indifferent good for either.
Here is a gentleman whom by chance I met,
Upon agreement from us to his liking,
Will undertake to woo curst Katharine,
Yea, and to marry her, if her dowry please. 185
    GREMIO
So said, so done, is well.
Hortensio, have you told him all her faults?
    PETRUCHIO
I know she is an irksome brawling scold:
If that be all masters, I hear no harm.
    GREMIO
No, sayst me so, friend? What countryman? 190
    PETRUCHIO
Born in Verona, old Antonio's son.
My father dead, my fortune lives for me,
And I do hope, good days and long to see.
    GREMIO
O sir, such a life, with such a wife, were strange.
But if you have a stomach, to't a God's name, 195
You shall have me assisting you in all.
But will you woo this wild-cat?
    PETRUCHIO

                        Will I live?
    GRUMIO
Will he woo her? Ay, or I'll hang her.
    PETRUCHIO
Why came I hither, but to that intent?
Think you a little din can daunt mine ears? 200
Have I not in my time heard lions roar?

Have I not heard the sea, puffed up with winds,
Rage like an angry boar, chafed with sweat?
Have I not heard great ordnance in the field,
And heaven's artillery thunder in the skies?   205
Have I not in a pitched battle heard
Loud 'larums, neighing steeds, and trumpet's
    clang?
And do you tell me of a woman's tongue,
That gives not half so great a blow to hear,
As will a chestnut in a farmer's fire?   210
Tush, tush, fear boys with bugs.

GRUMIO

                    For he fears none.

GREMIO

Hortensio hark.
This gentleman is happily arrived,
My mind presumes, for his own good, and yours.

HORTENSIO

I promised we would be contributors,   215
And bear his charge of wooing whatsoe'er.

GREMIO

And so we will, provided that he win her.

GRUMIO

I would I were as sure of a good dinner.

        Enter Tranio dressed as Lucentio, and
        Biondello.

TRANIO

Gentlemen God save you. If I may be bold,
Tell me I beseech you, which is the readiest way   220
To th' house of Signior Baptista Minola?

BIONDELLO

He that has the two fair daughters—is't he you
  mean?

TRANIO

Even he Biondello.

GREMIO

Hark you sir, you mean not her to—   225

TRANIO

Perhaps him and her sir, what have you to do?

PETRUCHIO

Not her that chides sir, at any hand I pray.

TRANIO

I love no chiders sir. Biondello, let's away.

LUCENTIO [*aside*]

Well begun Tranio.

HORTENSIO

                    Sir, a word ere you go.
Are you a suitor to the maid you talk of, yea or
  no?   230

TRANIO

An if I be sir, is it any offence?

GREMIO

No; if without more words you will get you
  hence.

TRANIO

Why, sir, I pray are not the streets as free
For me, as for you?

GREMIO

                    But so is not she.

TRANIO

For what reason I beseech you?

GREMIO

            For this reason if you'll know, 235
That she's the choice love of Signior Gremio.

HORTENSIO

That's she's the chosen of Signior Hortensio.

TRANIO

Softly my masters! If you be gentlemen,
Do me this right; hear me with patience.
Baptista is a noble gentleman, 240
To whom my father is not all unknown,
And were his daughter fairer than she is,
She may more suitors have, and me for one.
Fair Leda's daughter had a thousand wooers,
Then well one more may fair Bianca have; 245
And so she shall. Lucentio shall make one,
Though Paris came, in hope to speed alone.

GREMIO

What, this gentleman will out-talk us all.

LUCENTIO

Sir give him head, I know he'll prove a jade.

PETRUCHIO

Hortensio, to what end are all these words? 250

HORTENSIO

Sir, let me be so bold as ask you,
Did you yet ever see Baptista's daughter?

TRANIO

No sir, but hear I do that he hath two;
The one as famous for a scolding tongue,

As is the other, for beauteous modesty.   255
　　PETRUCHIO
Sir, sir, the first's for me, let her go by.
　　GREMIO
Yea, leave that labour to great Hercules,
And let it be more than Alcides' twelve.
　　PETRUCHIO
Sir understand you this of me, in sooth.
The youngest daughter whom you hearken for,   260
Her father keeps from all access of suitors,
And will not promise her to any man
Until the elder sister first be wed.
The younger then is free, and not before.
　　TRANIO
If it be so sir, that you are the man   265
Must stead us all, and me amongst the rest.
And if you break the ice, and do this feat,
Achieve the elder, set the younger free
For our access, whose hap shall be to have her
Will not so graceless be, to be ingrate.   270
　　HORTENSIO
Sir you say well, and well you do conceive,
And since you do profess to be a suitor,
You must, as we do, gratify this gentleman,
To whom we all rest generally beholding.
　　TRANIO
Sir, I shall not be slack; in sign whereof,   275
Please ye we may contrive this afternoon,
And quaff carouses to our mistress' health,
And do as adversaries do in law,

Strive mightily, but eat and drink as friends.

GRUMIO *and* BIONDELLO

O excellent motion! Fellows let's be gone.   280

HORTENSIO

The motion's good indeed, and be it so,
Petruchio, I shall be your ben venuto.   [*Exeunt.*

Act two Scene one

> *Padua. A room in Baptista's house. Enter Katharine, and Bianca with her hands bound.*

BIANCA

Good sister, wrong me not, nor wrong yourself,
To make a bondmaid and a slave of me—
That I disdain. But for these other gauds,
Unbind my hands, I'll put them off myself,
Yea all my raiment, to my petticoat,   5
Or what you will command me, will I do,
So well I know my duty to my elders.

KATHARINE

Of all thy suitors, here I charge thee, tell
Whom thou lov'st best. See thou dissemble not.

BIANCA

Believe me sister, of all the men alive,   10
I never yet beheld that special face,
Which I could fancy more than any other.

KATHARINE

Minion thou liest. Is't not Hortensio?

BIANCA

If you affect him sister, here I swear
I'll plead for you myself, but you shall have him.   15

KATHARINE

O then belike you fancy riches more;
You will have Gremio to keep you fair.

BIANCA

Is it for him you do envy me so?
Nay then you jest, and now I well perceive
You have but jested with me all this while.   20
I prithee sister Kate, untie my hands.

KATHARINE

If that be jest, then all the rest was so.

[*Strikes her.*

Enter Baptista.

BAPTISTA

Why how now dame, whence grows this inso-
    lence?
Bianca stand aside. Poor girl, she weeps.
Go ply thy needle, meddle not with her.   25
For shame thou hilding of a devilish spirit,
Why dost thou wrong her, that did ne'er wrong
    thee?
When did she cross thee with a bitter word?

KATHARINE

Her silence flouts me, and I'll be revenged.

[*Makes for Bianca.*

BAPTISTA [*holds her back*]

What, in my sight? Bianca get thee in.   30

[*Exit Bianca.*

KATHARINE

What will you not suffer me? Nay now I see
She is your treasure, she must have a husband;
I must dance barefoot on her wedding-day,
And for your love to her, lead apes in hell.
Talk not to me, I will go sit and weep,   35
Till I can find occasion of revenge.   [*Exit.*

BAPTISTA

Was ever gentleman thus grieved as I?

> *Enter Gremio, with Lucentio as Cam-*
> *bio; Petruchio, with Hortensio as Licio*
> *the musician; and Tranio as Lucentio,*
> *with Biondello bearing a lute and books.*

But who comes here?

GREMIO

Good morrow neighbour Baptista.

BAPTISTA

Good morrow neighbour Gremio. God save you   40
gentlemen.

PETRUCHIO

And you good sir. Pray have you not a daughter
Called Katharina, fair and virtuous?

BAPTISTA

I have a daughter sir, called Katharina.

GREMIO

You are too blunt, go to it orderly.   45

PETRUCHIO

You wrong me Signior Gremio, give me leave.
I am a gentleman of Verona sir,
That hearing of her beauty, and her wit,

Her affability and bashful modesty,
Her wondrous qualities, and mild behaviour,   50
Am bold to show myself a forward guest
Within your house, to make mine eye the witness
Of that report which I so oft have heard.
And for an entrance to my entertainment,
I do present you with a man of mine,   55

      [*Presents Hortensio.*

Cunning in music and the mathematics,
To instruct her fully in those sciences,
Whereof I know she is not ignorant.
Accept of him, or else you do me wrong.
His name is Licio, born in Mantua.   60

  BAPTISTA

You're welcome sir, and he for your good sake.
But for my daughter Katharine, this I know,
She is not for your turn, the more my grief.

  PETRUCHIO

I see you do not mean to part with her,
Or else you like not of my company.   65

  BAPTISTA

Mistake me not, I speak but as I find.
Whence are you sir? What may I call your name?

  PETRUCHIO

Petruchio is my name, Antonio's son,
A man well known throughout all Italy.

  BAPTISTA

I knew him well; you are welcome for his sake.   70

  GREMIO

Saving your tale Petruchio, I pray

Let us that are poor petitioners speak too.
Baccare! You are marvellous forward.

PETRUCHIO

O, pardon me Signior Gremio, I would fain be
doing.

GREMIO

I doubt it not sir, but you will curse your woo-
ing.   75
Neighbour, this is a gift very grateful, I am sure of
it. To express the like kindness myself, that have
been more kindly beholding to you than any, I
freely give unto you this young scholar [*presents
Lucentio*], that hath been long studying at   80
Rheims; as cunning in Greek, Latin, and other
languages, as the other in music and mathematics
—his name is Cambio; pray accept his service.

BAPTISTA

A thousand thanks Signior Gremio. Welcome   85
good Cambio. [*To Tranio.*] But gentle sir, methinks you walk like a stranger. May I be so bold
to know the cause of your coming?

TRANIO

Pardon me sir, the boldness is mine own,
That being a stranger in this city here,   90
Do make myself a suitor to your daughter,
Unto Bianca, fair and virtuous.
Nor is your firm resolve unknown to me,
In the preferment of the eldest sister.
This liberty is all that I request,   95
That upon knowledge of my parentage,

I may have welcome 'mongst the rest that woo,
And free access and favour as the rest.
And toward the education of your daughters,
I here bestow a simple instrument,   100
And this small packet of Greek and Latin
    books.
If you accept them, then their worth is great.
          BAPTISTA
Lucentio is your name—of whence I pray?
          TRANIO
Of Pisa sir, son to Vincentio.
          BAPTISTA
A mighty man of Pisa; by report   105
I know him well. You are very welcome sir.
[*To Hortensio.*] Take you the lute, [*to Lucen-
    tio*] and you the set of books.
You shall go see your pupils presently.
Holla, within!
          Enter a Servant.
                    Sirrah, lead these gentlemen
To my two daughters, and tell them both   110
These are their tutors; bid them use them well.
          [*Exit Servant, with Hortensio,
              Lucentio, and Biondello.*
We will go walk a little in the orchard,
And then to dinner. You are passing welcome,
And so I pray you all to think yourselves.
          PETRUCHIO
Signior Baptista, my business asketh haste,   115
And every day I cannot come to woo.

You knew my father well, and in him me,
Left solely heir to all his lands and goods,
Which I have bettered rather than decreased.
Then tell me, if I get your daughter's love,   120
What dowry shall I have with her to wife?

BAPTISTA

After my death, the one half of my lands,
And in possession twenty thousand crowns.

PETRUCHIO

And for that dowry, I'll assure her of
Her widowhood, be it that she survive me,   125
In all my lands and leases whatsoever.
Let specialties be therefore drawn between us,
That covenants may be kept on either hand.

BAPTISTA

Ay, when the special thing is well obtained,
That is, her love; for that is all in all.   130

PETRUCHIO

Why that is nothing; for I tell you father,
I am as peremptory as she proud-minded.
And where two raging fires meet together,
They do consume the thing that feeds their
          fury.
Though little fire grows great with little wind,   135
Yet extreme gusts will blow out fire and all.
So I to her, and so she yields to me,
For I am rough, and woo not like a babe.

BAPTISTA

Well mayst thou woo, and happy be thy speed.
But be thou armed for some unhappy words.   140

PETRUCHIO

Ay, to the proof, as mountains are for winds,
That shake not, though they blow perpetually.
        Enter Hortensio, with a wounded head.

BAPTISTA

How now my friend, why dost thou look so pale?

HORTENSIO

For fear, I promise you, if I look pale.

BAPTISTA

What, will my daughter prove a good musician?   145

HORTENSIO

I think she'll sooner prove a soldier.
Iron may hold with her, but never lutes.

BAPTISTA

Why then thou canst not break her to the lute?

HORTENSIO

Why no, for she hath broke the lute to me.
I did but tell her she mistook her frets,   150
And bowed her hand to teach her fingering;
When, with a most impatient devilish spirit,
Frets call you these? quoth she, I'll fume with
    them.
And with that word she struck me on the head,
And through the instrument my pate made way,   155
And there I stood amazed for a while,
As on a pillory, looking through the lute;
While she did call me rascal fiddler
And twangling Jack, with twenty such vile
    terms,
As had she studied to misuse me so.   160

PETRUCHIO

Now by the world, it is a lusty wench.
I love her ten times more than e'er I did.
O how I long to have some chat with her.

BAPTISTA

Well go with me, and be not so discomfited.
Proceed in practice with my younger daughter;   165
She's apt to learn, and thankful for good turns.
Signior Petruchio, will you go with us,
Or shall I send my daughter Kate to you?

PETRUCHIO

I pray you do. I will attend her here,

[*Exeunt Baptista, Gremio,
Tranio, and Hortensio.*

And woo her with some spirit when she comes.   170
Say that she rail, why then I'll tell her plain,
She sings as sweetly as a nightingale.
Say that she frown, I'll say she looks as clear
As morning roses newly washed with dew.
Say she be mute, and will not speak a word,   175
Then I'll commend her volubility,
And say she uttereth piercing eloquence.
If she do bid me pack, I'll give her thanks,
As though she bid me stay by her a week.
If she deny to wed, I'll crave the day   180
When I shall ask the banns, and when be mar-
    ried.

Enter Katharine.

But here she comes; and now Petruchio, speak.
Good morrow Kate, for that's your name I hear.

KATHARINE

Well have you heard, but something hard of
    hearing;
They call me Katharine, that do talk of me.   185

PETRUCHIO

You lie in faith, for you are called plain Kate,
And bonny Kate, and sometimes Kate the curst.
But Kate, the prettiest Kate in Christendom,
Kate of Kate-Hall, my super-dainty Kate,
For dainties are all Kates, and therefore Kate,   190
Take this of me, Kate of my consolation—
Hearing thy mildness praised in every town,
Thy virtues spoke of, and thy beauty sounded,
Yet not so deeply as to thee belongs,
Myself am moved to woo thee for my wife.   195

KATHARINE

Moved? In good time. Let him that moved you
    hither
Remove you hence; I knew you at the first
You were a moveable.

PETRUCHIO

                  Why, what's a moveable?

KATHARINE

A joint-stool.

PETRUCHIO

         Thou hast hit it. Come sit on me.

KATHARINE

Asses are made to bear, and so are you.   200

PETRUCHIO

Women are made to bear, and so are you.

KATHARINE

No such jade as you, if me you mean.

PETRUCHIO

Alas good Kate, I will not burthen thee.
For knowing thee to be but young and light—

KATHARINE

Too light for such a swain as you to catch,   205
And yet as heavy as my weight should be.

PETRUCHIO

Should be? Should—buzz!

KATHARINE

       Well ta'en, and like a buzzard.

PETRUCHIO

O slow-winged turtle, shall a buzzard take thee?

KATHARINE

Ay, for a turtle, as he takes a buzzard.

PETRUCHIO

Come, come, you wasp, i' faith you are too
   angry.   210

KATHARINE

If I be waspish, best beware my sting.

PETRUCHIO

My remedy is then to pluck it out.

KATHARINE

Ay, if the fool could find it where it lies.

PETRUCHIO

Who knows not where a wasp does wear his
   sting?
In his tail.   215

KATHARINE

In his tongue.

PETRUCHIO

Whose tongue?

KATHARINE

Yours if you talk of tails, and so farewell.

PETRUCHIO

What, with my tongue in your tail? Nay, come
again.

Good Kate, I am a gentleman.

KATHARINE

That I'll try.　220
[*She strikes him.*

PETRUCHIO

I swear I'll cuff you, if you strike again.

KATHARINE

So may you lose your arms.

If you strike me, you are no gentleman;

And if no gentleman, why then no arms.

PETRUCHIO

A herald Kate? O put me in thy books.　225

KATHARINE

What is your crest, a coxcomb?

PETRUCHIO

A combless cock, so Kate will be my hen.

KATHARINE

No cock of mine, you crow too like a craven.

PETRUCHIO

Nay come Kate, come, you must not look so
sour.

KATHARINE

It is my fashion when I see a crab.   23

PETRUCHIO

Why here's no crab, and therefore look not sour.

KATHARINE

There is, there is.

PETRUCHIO

Then show it me.

KATHARINE

       Had I a glass, I would.

PETRUCHIO

What, you mean my face?   23

KATHARINE

       Well aimed of such a young one.

PETRUCHIO

Now by Saint George I am too young for you.

KATHARINE

Yet you are withered.

PETRUCHIO

       'Tis with cares.   24

KATHARINE

             I care not.

PETRUCHIO

Nay hear you Kate. In sooth you 'scape not so.

KATHARINE

I chafe you if I tarry. Let me go.

PETRUCHIO

No, not a whit; I find you passing gentle.

'Twas told me you were rough, and coy, and
   sullen,   24

And now I find report a very liar.
For thou art pleasant, gamesome, passing cour-
  teous,
But slow in speech, yet sweet as spring-time
  flowers.
Thou canst not frown, thou canst not look
  askance,
Nor bite the lip, as angry wenches will;   250
Nor hast thou pleasure to be cross in talk.
But thou with mildness entertain'st thy wooers,
With gentle conference, soft, and affable.
Why does the world report that Kate doth limp?
O slanderous world, Kate like a hazel-twig   255
Is straight, and slender, and as brown in hue
As hazel-nuts, and sweeter than the kernels.
O let me see thee walk. Thou dost not halt.

> KATHARINE

Go fool, and whom thou keep'st, command.

> PETRUCHIO

Did ever Dian so become a grove   260
As Kate this chamber with her princely gait?
O be thou Dian, and let her be Kate;
And then let Kate be chaste, and Dian sportful.

> KATHARINE

Where did you study all this goodly speech?

> PETRUCHIO

It is extempore, from my mother-wit.   265

> KATHARINE

A witty mother, witless else her son.

PETRUCHIO

Am I not wise?

KATHARINE

Yes, keep you warm.

PETRUCHIO

Marry so I mean, sweet Katharine, in thy bed.
And therefore, setting all this chat aside,   270
Thus in plain terms—your father hath consented
That you shall be my wife; your dowry 'greed on;
And will you, nill you, I will marry you.
Now Kate, I am a husband for your turn,
For by this light, whereby I see thy beauty,   275
Thy beauty that doth make me like thee well,
Thou must be married to no man but me.
For I am he am born to tame you Kate,
And bring you from a wild Kate to a Kate
Conformable as other household Kates.   280
        Enter Baptista, Gremio, and Tranio.
Here comes your father. Never make denial;
I must, and will have Katharine to my wife.

BAPTISTA

Now Signior Petruchio, how speed you with my
    daughter?

PETRUCHIO

How but well sir? How but well?
It were impossible I should speed amiss.   285

BAPTISTA

Why how now daughter Katharine? In your
    dumps?

KATHARINE

Call you me daughter? Now I promise you,
You have showed a tender fatherly regard,
To wish me wed to one half lunatic,
A mad-cap ruffian, and a swearing Jack,   290
That thinks with oaths to face the matter out.

PETRUCHIO

Father, 'tis thus—yourself and all the world
That talked of her, have talked amiss of her.
If she be curst, it is for policy,
For she's not froward, but modest as the dove.   295
She is not hot, but temperate as the morn.
For patience she will prove a second Grissel,
And Roman Lucrece for her chastity.
And to conclude, we have 'greed so well to-
    gether,
That upon Sunday is the wedding-day.   300

KATHARINE

I'll see thee hanged on Sunday first.

GREMIO

Hark Petruchio, she says she'll see thee hanged
    first.

TRANIO

Is this your speeding? Nay then good night our
    part.

PETRUCHIO

Be patient gentlemen, I choose her for myself.
If she and I be pleased, what's that to you?   305
'Tis bargained 'twixt us twain, being alone,
That she shall still be curst in company.

I tell you 'tis incredible to believe
How much she loves me: o the kindest Kate!
She hung about my neck, and kiss on kiss   310
She vied so fast, protesting oath on oath,
That in a twink she won me to her love.
O you are novices, 'tis a world to see
How tame when men and women are alone,
A meacock wretch can make the curstest shrew.   315
Give me thy hand Kate, I will unto Venice,
To buy apparel 'gainst the wedding-day.
Provide the feast father, and bid the guests.
I will be sure my Katharine shall be fine.

BAPTISTA

I know not what to say—but give me your
    hands.   320
God send you joy, Petruchio, 'tis a match.

GREMIO *and* TRANIO

Amen say we; we will be witnesses.

PETRUCHIO

Father, and wife, and gentlemen, adieu.
I will to Venice; Sunday comes apace.
We will have rings, and things, and fine array;   325
[*Sings.*] *And kiss me Kate, we will be married o'*
    Sunday.

    [*Exeunt Petruchio and Katharine severally.*

GREMIO

Was ever match clapped up so suddenly?

BAPTISTA

Faith gentlemen, now I play a merchant's part,
And venture madly on a desperate mart.

TRANIO
'Twas a commodity lay fretting by you.   330
'Twill bring you gain, or perish on the seas.

BAPTISTA
The gain I seek is, quiet in the match.

GREMIO
No doubt but he hath got a quiet catch.
But now Baptista, to your younger daughter.
Now is the day we long have looked for.   335
I am your neighbour, and was suitor first.

TRANIO
And I am one that love Bianca more
Than words can witness, or your thoughts can
     guess.

GREMIO
Youngling, thou canst not love so dear as I.

TRANIO
Greybeard, thy love doth freeze.

GREMIO
                                        But thine doth fry, 340
Skipper stand back, 'tis age that nourisheth.

TRANIO
But youth in ladies' eyes that flourisheth.

BAPTISTA
Content you gentlemen, I will compound this
     strife.
'Tis deeds must win the prize, and he of both
That can assure my daughter greatest dower,   345
Shall have my Bianca's love.
Say Signior Gremio, what can you assure her?

GREMIO

First, as you know, my house within the city,
Is richly furnished with plate and gold,
Basins and ewers, to lave her dainty hands;   350
My hangings all of Tyrian tapestry;
In ivory coffers I have stuffed my crowns;
In cypress chests my arras counterpoints,
Costly apparel, tents, and canopies,
Fine linen, Turkey cushions bossed with pearl,   355
Valance of Venice gold in needlework;
Pewter and brass, and all things that belong
To house or housekeeping. Then at my farm
I have a hundred milch kine to the pail,
Six score fat oxen standing in my stalls,   360
And all things answerable to this portion.
Myself am struck in years I must confess;
And if I die to-morrow this is hers,
If whilst I live she will be only mine.

TRANIO

That only came well in. Sir, list to me.   365
I am my father's heir and only son.
If I may have your daughter to my wife,
I'll leave her houses three or four as good,
Within rich Pisa walls, as any one
Old Signior Gremio has in Padua;   370
Besides, two thousand ducats by the year
Of fruitful land, all which shall be her jointure.
What, have I pinched you Signior Gremio?

GREMIO

Two thousand ducats by the year of land!

My land amounts but to so much in all.   375
That she shall have, besides an argosy
That now is lying in Marseilles' road.
What, have I choked you with an argosy?

TRANIO

Gremio, 'tis known my father hath no less
Than three great argosies, besides two galliasses,   380
And twelve tight galleys. These I will assure her,
And twice as much whate'er thou offer'st next.

GREMIO

Nay, I have offered all, I have no more,
And she can have no more than all I have.
If you like me, she shall have me and mine.   385

TRANIO

Why then the maid is mine from all the world
By your firm promise. Gremio is out-vied.

BAPTISTA

I must confess your offer is the best,
And let your father make her the assurance,
She is your own, else you must pardon me.   390
If you should die before him, where's her dower?

TRANIO

That's but a cavil. He is old, I young.

GREMIO

And may not young men die as well as old?

BAPTISTA

Well gentlemen,
I am thus resolved. On Sunday next, you know   395
My daughter Katharine is to be married.
Now on the Sunday following, shall Bianca

Be bride to you, if you make this assurance;
If not, to Signior Gremio.
And so I take my leave, and thank you both.   400

GREMIO

Adieu good neighbour.   [*Exit Baptista.*
                    Now I fear thee not.
Sirrah, young gamester, your father were a fool
To give thee all, and in his waning age
Set foot under thy table. Tut, a toy;
An old Italian fox is not so kind, my boy.   [*Exit.*   405

TRANIO

A vengeance on your crafty withered hide.
Yet I have faced it with a card of ten.
'Tis in my head to do my master good.
I see no reason but supposed Lucentio
Must get a father, called supposed Vincentio;   410
And that's a wonder. Fathers commonly
Do get their children; but in this case of wooing,
A child shall get a sire, if I fail not of my cun-
    ning.   [*Exit.*

Act three Scene one

> *Padua. A room in Baptista's house. Enter*
> *Lucentio as Cambio, Hortensio as Licio,*
> *and Bianca.*

LUCENTIO

Fiddler forbear; you grow too forward sir.
Have you so soon forgot the entertainment
Her sister Katharine welcomed you withal?

HORTENSIO

But wrangling pedant, this is
The patroness of heavenly harmony.	5
Then give me leave to have prerogative,
And when in music we have spent an hour,
Your lecture shall have leisure for as much.

LUCENTIO

Preposterous ass, that never read so far,
To know the cause why music was ordained.	10
Was it not to refresh the mind of man
After his studies, or his usual pain?
Then give me leave to read philosophy,
And while I pause, serve in your harmony.

HORTENSIO

Sirrah, I will not bear these braves of thine.	15

BIANCA

Why gentlemen, you do me double wrong,
To strive for that which resteth in my choice.
I am no breeching scholar in the schools;
I'll not be tied to hours, nor 'pointed times,
But learn my lessons as I please myself.	20
And, to cut off all strife, here sit we down.
Take you your instrument, play you the whiles,
His lecture will be done ere you have tuned.

HORTENSIO

You'll leave his lecture when I am in tune?

LUCENTIO

That will be never. Tune your instrument.	25

[Hortensio retires.

BIANCA

Where left we last?

LUCENTIO

Here madam.   [*Reads.*
          Hic ibat Simois, hic est Sigeia tellus,
               Hic steterat Priami regia celsa senis.

BIANCA

Conster them.   30

LUCENTIO

Hic ibat, as I told you before—*Simois*, I am
Lucentio—*hic est*, son unto Vincentio of Pisa—
Sigeia tellus, disguised thus to get your love—
Hic steterat, and that Lucentio that comes a-woo-
ing—*Priami*, is my man Tranio—*regia*, bearing   35
my port—*celsa senis*, that we might beguile the
old pantaloon.

HORTENSIO [*comes forward*].

Madam, my instrument's in tune.

BIANCA

                    Let's hear.   [*He plays.*
O fie, the treble jars.

LUCENTIO

                    Spit in the hole man,
And tune again.   40

BIANCA

Now let me see if I can conster it.
Hic ibat Simois, I know you not—*hic est Sigeia
tellus*, I trust you not—*Hic steterat Priami*, take
heed he hear us not—*regia*, presume not—*celsa
senis*, despair not.   45

HORTENSIO

Madam, 'tis now in tune.

LUCENTIO

All but the base.

HORTENSIO

The base is right, 'tis the base knave that jars.
[*Aside*.] How fiery and forward our pedant is.
Now for my life the knave doth court my love.
Pedascule, I'll watch you better yet.   50

BIANCA

In time I may believe, yet I mistrust.

LUCENTIO

Mistrust it not, for sure Aeacides
Was Ajax, called so from his grandfather.

BIANCA

I must believe my master, else I promise you,
I should be arguing still upon that doubt.   55
But let it rest. Now Licio to you.
Good masters, take it not unkindly pray,
That I have been thus pleasant with you both.

HORTENSIO [*to Lucentio*]

You may go walk, and give me leave awhile.
My lessons make no music in three parts.   60

LUCENTIO

Are you so formal, sir? Well I must wait—
[*Aside*.] And watch withal, for but I be deceived,
Our fine musician groweth amorous.

HORTENSIO

Madam, before you touch the instrument,
To learn the order of my fingering,   65

I must begin with rudiments of art,
To teach you gamut in a briefer sort,
More pleasant, pithy, and effectual,
Than hath been taught by any of my trade.
And there it is in writing, fairly drawn.   70

BIANCA

Why, I am past my gamut long ago.

HORTENSIO

Yet read the gamut of Hortensio.

BIANCA [*reads*]

Gamut *I am, the ground of all accord.*
A re, *to plead Hortensio's passion;*
B mi, *Bianca, take him for thy lord,*   75
C fa ut, *that loves with all affection.*
D sol re, *one clef, two notes have I;*
E la mi, *show pity or I die.*

Call you this gamut? Tut I like it not.
Old fashions please me best; I am not so nice   80
To change true rules for odd inventions.

Enter a servant.

SERVANT

Mistress, your father prays you leave your books,
And help to dress your sister's chamber up.
You know to-morrow is the wedding-day.

BIANCA

Farewell sweet masters both, I must be gone.   85

[*Exeunt Bianca and Servant.*

LUCENTIO

Faith mistress, then I have no cause to stay.

[*Exit.*

HORTENSIO

But I have cause to pry into this pedant;
Methinks he looks as though he were in love.
Yet if thy thoughts, Bianca, be so humble,
To cast thy wandering eyes on every stale,   90
Seize thee that list. If once I find thee ranging,
Hortensio will be quit with thee by changing.

[*Exit.*

Scene two

> *The same. The Square, before Baptista's*
> *house. Enter Baptista, Gremio, Tranio as*
> *Lucentio, Katharine, Bianca, Lucentio*
> *as Cambio, and others, with Attendants.*

BAPTISTA [*to Tranio*].

Signior Lucentio, this is the 'pointed day
That Katharine and Petruchio should be mar-
    ried,
And yet we hear not of our son-in-law.
What will be said? What mockery will it be,
To want the bridegroom when the priest attends   5
To speak the ceremonial rites of marriage.
What says Lucentio to this shame of ours?

KATHARINE

No shame but mine. I must forsooth be forced
To give my hand, opposed against my heart,
Unto a mad-brain rudesby, full of spleen,   10

Who wooed in haste, and means to wed at lei-
  sure.
I told you, I, he was a frantic fool,
Hiding his bitter jests in blunt behaviour;
And to be noted for a merry man,
He'll woo as husband, 'point the day of marriage,   15
Make feast, invite friends, and proclaim the
  banns,
Yet never means to wed where he hath wooed.
Now must the world point at poor Katharine,
And say, lo, there is mad Petruchio's wife,
If it would please him come and marry her.   20

TRANIO
Patience good Katharine, and Baptista too.
Upon my life Petruchio means but well,
Whatever fortune stays him from his word.
Though he be blunt, I know him passing wise;
Though he be merry, yet withal he's honest.   25

KATHARINE
Would Katharine had never seen him though.
  [*Exit weeping, followed by Bianca and others.*

BAPTISTA
Go girl, I cannot blame thee now to weep,
For such an injury would vex a saint,
Much more a shrew of thy impatient humour.
    Enter Biondello.

BIONDELLO
Master, master, old news! And such news as you   30
never heard of!

BAPTISTA

Is it new and old too? How may that be?

BIONDELLO

Why, is it not news to hear of Petruchio's coming?

BAPTISTA

Is he come?   35

BIONDELLO

Why no sir.

BAPTISTA

What then?

BIONDELLO

He is coming.

BAPTISTA

When will he be here?

BIONDELLO

When he stands where I am, and sees you there.   40

TRANIO

But say, what to thine old news?

BIONDELLO

Why Petruchio is coming, in a new hat and an
old jerkin; a pair of old breeches thrice turned; a
pair of boots that have been candle-cases, one   45
buckled, another laced; an old rusty sword ta'en
out of the town armoury, with a broken hilt, and
chapeless; with two broken points; his horse
hipped—with an old mothy saddle, and stirrups
of no kindred—besides, possessed with the glan-   50
ders, and like to mose in the chine; troubled with
the lampass, infected with the fashions, full of

windgalls, sped with spavins, rayed with the yellows, past cure of the fives, stark spoiled with the staggers, begnawn with the bots; swayed in the back, and shoulder-shotten; near-legged before, and with a half-cheeked bit, and a headstall of sheep's leather, which being restrained to keep him from stumbling, hath been often burst, and new-repaired with knots; one girth six times pieced, and a woman's crupper of velure, which hath two letters for her name, fairly set down in studs, and here and there pieced with pack-thread. 55 60

BAPTISTA

Who comes with him? 65

BIONDELLO

O sir, his lackey, for all the world caparisoned like the horse; with a linen stock on one leg, and a kersey boot-hose on the other, gartered with a red and blue list; an old hat, and the humour of forty fancies pricked in't for a feather: a monster, a very monster in apparel, and not like a Christian footboy or a gentleman's lackey. 70

TRANIO

'Tis some odd humour pricks him to this fashion.
Yet oftentimes he goes but mean-apparelled. 75

BAPTISTA

I am glad he's come, howsoe'er he comes.

BIONDELLO

Why sir, he comes not.

BAPTISTA

Didst thou not say he comes?

BIONDELLO

Who? That Petruchio came?

BAPTISTA

Ay, that Petruchio came. 80

BIONDELLO

No sir, I say his horse comes, with him on his
back.

BAPTISTA

Why that's all one.

BIONDELLO [*sings*]

   Nay by Saint Jamy,
   I hold you a penny,
   A horse and a man 85
   Is more than one,
   And yet not many.

Enter Petruchio and Grumio.

PETRUCHIO

Come, where be these gallants? Who's at home?

BAPTISTA

You're welcome sir.

PETRUCHIO

And yet I come not well. 90

BAPTISTA

And yet you halt not.

TRANIO

Not so well apparelled as I wish you were.

PETRUCHIO

Were it not better I should rush in thus?

But where is Kate? Where is my lovely bride?
How does my father? Gentles methinks you
   frown.   95
And wherefore gaze this goodly company,
As if they saw some wondrous monument,
Some comet, or unusual prodigy?

   BAPTISTA

Why sir, you know this is your wedding-day.
First we were sad, fearing you would not come,   100
Now sadder that you come so unprovided.
Fie, doff this habit, shame to your estate,
An eye-sore to our solemn festival.

   TRANIO

And tell us what occasion of import
Hath all so long detained you from your wife,   105
And sent you hither so unlike yourself?

   PETRUCHIO

Tedious it were to tell, and harsh to hear.
Sufficeth I am come to keep my word,
Though in some part enforced to digress,
Which at more leisure I will so excuse,   110
As you shall well be satisfied withal.
But where is Kate? I stay too long from her.
The morning wears, 'tis time we were at church.

   TRANIO

See not your bride in these unreverent robes.
Go to my chamber, put on clothes of mine.   115

   PETRUCHIO

Not I, believe me. Thus I'll visit her.

BAPTISTA

But thus I trust you will not marry her.

PETRUCHIO

Good sooth even thus. Therefore ha' done with
    words;
To me she's married, not unto my clothes.
Could I repair what she will wear in me,   120
As I can change these poor accoutrements,
'Twere well for Kate, and better for myself.
But what a fool am I to chat with you,
When I should bid good morrow to my bride,
And seal the title with a lovely kiss.   125
            [*Exeunt Petruchio and Grumio.*

TRANIO

He hath some meaning in his mad attire.
We will persuade him, be it possible,
To put on better ere he go to church.

BAPTISTA

I'll after him, and see the event of this.
    [*Exeunt Baptista, Gremio, and Attendants.*

TRANIO

But sir, to love concerneth us to add   130
Her father's liking, which to bring to pass,
As I before imparted to your worship,
I am to get a man—whate'er he be,
It skills not much, we'll fit him to our turn—
And he shall be Vincentio of Pisa,   135
And make assurance here in Padua
Of greater sums than I have promised.
So shall you quietly enjoy your hope,

And marry sweet Bianca with consent.

LUCENTIO

Were it not that my fellow-schoolmaster 140
Doth watch Bianca's steps so narrowly,
'Twere good methinks to steal our marriage,
Which once performed, let all the world say no,
I'll keep mine own despite of all the world.

TRANIO

That by degrees we mean to look into, 145
And watch our vantage in this business.
We'll over-reach the greybeard Gremio,
The narrow-prying father Minola,
The quaint musician, amorous Licio;
All for my master's sake, Lucentio. 150

Enter Gremio.

Signior Gremio, came you from the church?

GREMIO

As willingly as e'er I came from school.

TRANIO

And is the bride and bridegroom coming home?

GREMIO

A bridegroom say you? 'Tis a groom indeed,
A grumbling groom, and that the girl shall find. 155

TRANIO

Curster than she? Why 'tis impossible.

GREMIO

Why he's a devil, a devil, a very fiend.

TRANIO

Why she's a devil, a devil, the devil's dam.

GREMIO

Tut, she's a lamb, a dove, a fool to him.
I'll tell you Sir Lucentio—when the priest   160
Should ask if Katharine should be his wife,
Ay, by gogs-wouns, quoth he, and swore so loud,
That all amazed the priest let fall the book,
And as he stooped again to take it up,
This mad-brained bridegroom took him such a cuff,   165
That down fell priest and book, and book and priest.
Now take them up quoth he, if any list.

TRANIO

What said the wench when he rose again?

GREMIO

Trembled and shook. For why, he stamped and swore,
As if the vicar meant to cozen him.   170
But after many ceremonies done,
He calls for wine. A health quoth he, as if
He had been aboard, carousing to his mates
After a storm; quaffed off the muscadel,
And threw the sops all in the sexton's face;   175
Having no other reason,
But that his beard grew thin and hungerly,
And seemed to ask him sops as he was drinking.
This done, he took the bride about the neck,
And kissed her lips with such a clamorous smack,   180

That at the parting all the church did echo.
And I seeing this, came thence for very shame;
And after me I know the rout is coming.
Such a mad marriage never was before.
Hark, hark I hear the minstrels play.   185

> *Enter minstrels playing, cross the stage,*
> *and exeunt. Enter Petruchio, Katharine,*
> *Bianca, Baptista, Hortensio, Grumio,*
> *and Attendants.*

PETRUCHIO

Gentlemen and friends, I thank you for your
    pains.
I know you think to dine with me to-day,
And have prepared great store of wedding cheer.
But so it is, my haste doth call me hence,
And therefore here I mean to take my leave.   190

BAPTISTA

Is't possible you will away to-night?

PETRUCHIO

I must away to-day before night come.
Make it no wonder. If you knew my business,
You would entreat me rather go than stay.
And, honest company, I thank you all,   195
That have beheld me give away myself
To this most patient, sweet, and virtuous wife.
Dine with my father, drink a health to me,
For I must hence; and farewell to you all.

TRANIO

Let us entreat you stay till after dinner.

PETRUCHIO

It may not be.

GREMIO

    Let me entreat you. 200

PETRUCHIO

It cannot be.

KATHARINE

    Let me entreat you.

PETRUCHIO

I am content.

KATHARINE

    Are you content to stay?

PETRUCHIO

I am content you shall entreat me stay, 205
But yet not stay, entreat me how you can.

KATHARINE

Now if you love me stay.

PETRUCHIO

        Grumio, my horse.

GRUMIO

Ay sir, they be ready, the oats have eaten the
  horses.

KATHARINE

Nay then,
Do what thou canst, I will not go to-day, 210
No, nor to-morrow—not till I please myself.
The door is open sir, there lies your way;
You may be jogging whiles your boots are green.
For me, I'll not be gone till I please myself.
'Tis like you'll prove a jolly surly groom, 215

That take it on you at the first so roundly.

PETRUCHIO

O Kate content thee, prithee be not angry.

KATHARINE

I will be angry, what hast thou to do?
Father, be quiet, he shall stay my leisure.

GREMIO

Ay marry sir, now it begins to work.   220

KATHARINE

Gentlemen, forward to the bridal dinner.
I see a woman may be made a fool,
If she had not a spirit to resist.

PETRUCHIO

They shall go forward Kate, at thy command.
Obey the bride, you that attend on her.   225
Go to the feast, revel and domineer,
Carouse full measure to her maidenhead,
Be mad and merry, or go hang yourselves.
But for my bonny Kate, she must with me.
Nay, look not big, nor stamp, nor stare, nor fret;   230
I will be master of what is mine own.
She is my goods, my chattels; she is my house,
My household stuff, my field, my barn,
My horse, my ox, my ass, my any thing.
And here she stands, touch her whoever dare.   235
I'll bring mine action on the proudest he
That stops my way in Padua. Grumio,
Draw forth thy weapon, we are beset with
     thieves.
Rescue thy mistress if thou be a man.

Fear not sweet wench, they shall not touch thee,
   Kate.   240

I'll buckler thee against a million.
    [Exeunt Petruchio, Katharine, and Grumio.

    BAPTISTA

Nay let them go, a couple of quiet ones.

    GREMIO

Went they not quickly, I should die with
   laughing.

    TRANIO

Of all mad matches never was the like.

    LUCENTIO

Mistress, what's your opinion of your sister?   245

    BIANCA

That being mad herself, she's madly mated.

    GREMIO

I warrant him Petruchio is Kated.

    BAPTISTA

Neighbours and friends, though bride and bridegroom wants

For to supply the places at the table,

You know there wants no junkets at the feast.   250

Lucentio, you shall supply the bridegroom's
   place,

And let Bianca take her sister's room.

    TRANIO

Shall sweet Bianca practise how to bride it?

    BAPTISTA

She shall, Lucentio. Come gentlemen, let's go.
                    [Exeunt.

Act four Scene one

Petrucio's country house.
Enter Grumio.

GRUMIO

Fie, fie on all tired jades, on all mad masters, and
all foul ways! Was ever man so beaten? Was ever
man so rayed? Was ever man so weary? I am sent
before to make a fire, and they are coming after
to warm them. Now were not I a little pot, and   5
soon hot, my very lips might freeze to my teeth,
my tongue to the roof of my mouth, my heart in
my belly, ere I should come by a fire to thaw me;
but I with blowing the fire shall warm myself,   10
for considering the weather, a taller man than I
will take cold. Holla, ho Curtis!

Enter Curtis.

CURTIS

Who is that calls so coldly?

GRUMIO

A piece of ice. If thou doubt it, thou mayst slide
from my shoulder to my heel, with no greater a   15
run but my head and my neck. A fire good
Curtis.

CURTIS

Is my master and his wife coming Grumio?

GRUMIO

O ay, Curtis ay, and therefore fire, fire; cast on   20
no water.

CURTIS

Is she so hot a shrew as she's reported?

GRUMIO

She was, good Curtis, before this frost. But thou
know'st winter tames man, woman and beast;
for it hath tamed my old master, and my new 25
mistress, and myself, fellow Curtis.

CURTIS

Away you three-inch fool! I am no beast.

GRUMIO

Am I but three inches? Why thy horn is a foot,
and so long am I at the least. But wilt thou make 30
a fire, or shall I complain on thee to our mistress,
whose hand—she being now at hand—thou shalt
soon feel, to thy cold comfort, for being slow in
thy hot office?

CURTIS

I prithee good Grumio, tell me, how goes the 35
world?

GRUMIO

A cold world Curtis in every office but thine,
and therefore fire. Do thy duty, and have thy
duty, for my master and mistress are almost
frozen to death. 40

CURTIS

There's fire ready, and therefore good Grumio
the news?

GRUMIO

Why [*sings*] *Jack boy, ho boy*—and as much
news as thou wilt.

CURTIS

Come, you are so full of cony-catching.   45

GRUMIO

Why therefore fire, for I have caught extreme
cold. Where's the cook? Is supper ready, the
house trimmed, rushes strewed, cobwebs swept,
the serving men in their new fustian, their white
stockings, and every officer his wedding garment   50
on? Be the Jacks fair within, the Jills fair without, the carpets laid, and everything in order?

CURTIS

All ready; and therefore I pray thee, news.   55

GRUMIO

First know my horse is tired, my master and
mistress fallen out.

CURTIS

How?

GRUMIO

Out of their saddles into the dirt, and thereby
hangs a tale.   60

CURTIS

Let's ha't good Grumio.

GRUMIO

Lend thine ear.

CURTIS

Here.

GRUMIO

There.   [*Cuffs him*.

CURTIS

This 'tis to feel a tale, not to hear a tale.   65

GRUMIO

And therefore 'tis called a sensible tale; and this
cuff was but to knock at your ear, and beseech
listening. Now I begin, imprimis we came down
a foul hill, my master riding behind my mis-   70
tress—

CURTIS

Both of one horse?

GRUMIO

What's that to thee?

CURTIS

Why a horse.

GRUMIO

Tell thou the tale—but hadst thou not crossed
me, thou shouldst have heard how her horse fell,   75
and she under her horse; thou shouldst have
heard in how miry a place; how she was bemoiled, how he left her with the horse upon her,
how he beat me because her horse stumbled, how
she waded through the dirt to pluck him off me;   80
how he swore, how she prayed, that never prayed
before; how I cried, how the horses ran away,
how her bridle was burst; how I lost my crupper,
with many things of worthy memory, which now
shall die in oblivion, and thou return unexperi-   85
enced to thy grave.

CURTIS

By this reck'ning, he is more shrew than she.

GRUMIO

Ay, and that thou and the proudest of you all

shall find when he comes home. But what talk 90
I of this? Call forth Nathaniel, Joseph, Nicholas, Philip, Walter, Sugarsop and the rest. Let
their heads be slickly combed, their blue coats
brushed, and their garters of an indifferent knit.
Let them curtsy with their left legs, and not pre- 95
sume to touch a hair of my master's horse-tail,
till they kiss their hands. Are they all ready?

CURTIS

They are.

GRUMIO

Call them forth.

CURTIS

Do you hear, ho? You must meet my master to 100
countenance my mistress.

GRUMIO

Why she hath a face of her own.

CURTIS

Who knows not that?

GRUMIO

Thou it seems, that calls for company to countenance her. 105

CURTIS

I call them forth to credit her.

GRUMIO

Why she comes to borrow nothing of them.
Enter Servants.

NATHANIEL

Welcome home Grumio.

PHILIP

How now Grumio.   110

JOSEPH

What Grumio.

NICHOLAS

Fellow Grumio.

NATHANIEL

How now old lad.

GRUMIO

Welcome you—how now you—what you—fellow you—and thus much for greeting. Now my   115
spruce companions, is all ready, and all things
neat?

NATHANIEL

All things is ready. How near is our master?

GRUMIO

E'en at hand, alighted by this. And therefore be   120
not—Cock's passion, silence, I hear my master.

Enter Petruchio and Katharine.

PETRUCHIO

Where be these knaves? What, no man at door
To hold my stirrup, nor to take my horse?
Where is Nathaniel, Gregory, Philip?   125

ALL SERVANTS

Here, here sir, here sir.

PETRUCHIO

Here sir, here sir, here sir, here sir!
You logger-headed and unpolished grooms.
What, no attendance? No regard? No duty?
Where is the foolish knave I sent before?   130

GRUMIO

Here sir, as foolish as I was before.

PETRUCHIO

You peasant swain, you whoreson malt-horse
    drudge!
Did I not bid thee meet me in the park,
And bring along these rascal knaves with thee?

GRUMIO

Nathaniel's coat sir, was not fully made,   135
And Gabriel's pumps were all unpinked i' th'
    heel.
There was no link to colour Peter's hat,
And Walter's dagger was not come from
    sheathing.
There were none fine, but Adam, Rafe, and
    Gregory;
The rest were ragged, old, and beggarly,   140
Yet as they are, here are they come to meet you.

PETRUCHIO

Go rascals, go, and fetch my supper in.
                              [*Exeunt Servants.*
[*Sings.*] *Where is the life that late I led?*
Where are those—Sit down Kate, and welcome.
Food, food, food, food!   145
            Enter servants with supper.
Why, when I say? Nay good sweet Kate be
    merry.
Off with my boots, you rogues. You villains,
    when?

[*Sings.*] It was the friar of orders gray,
      As he forth walked on his way—
Out you rogue, you pluck my foot awry.   ₁₅₀
Take that, and mend the plucking off the other.
                    [*Strikes him.*
Be merry Kate. Some water here. What ho!
      Enter Servant with water.
Where's my spaniel Troilus? Sirrah, get you
   hence,
And bid my cousin Ferdinand come hither.
                [*Exit another Servant.*
One, Kate, that you must kiss, and be acquainted
   with.   ₁₅₅
Where are my slippers? Shall I have some water?
Come Kate and wash, and welcome heartily.
You whoreson villain, will you let it fall?
                    [*Strikes him.*

    KATHARINE
Patience I pray you, 'twas a fault unwilling.

    PETRUCHIO
A whoreson beetle-headed, flap-eared knave!   ₁₆₀
Come Kate, sit down, I know you have a stom-
   ach.
Will you give thanks, sweet Kate, or else shall I?
What's this, mutton?

    FIRST SERVANT
            Ay.

    PETRUCHIO
                 Who brought it?

PETER

I.   ..

PETRUCHIO

'Tis burnt, and so is all the meat.
What dogs are these! Where is the rascal cook? 165
How durst you villains bring it from the dresser,
And serve it thus to me that love it not?
There, take it to you, trenchers, cups, and all.

> [*Throws the meat, &c., at them.*

You heedless joltheads and unmannered slaves!
What, do you grumble? I'll be with you straight. 170

> [*Exeunt Servants pursued by Petruchio.*

KATHARINE

I pray you husband, be not so disquiet.
The meat was well, if you were so contented.

PETRUCHIO

I tell thee Kate, 'twas burnt and dried away,
And I expressly am forbid to touch it,
For it engenders choler, planteth anger; 175
And better 'twere that both of us did fast,
Since of ourselves, ourselves are choleric,
Than feed it with such over-roasted flesh.
Be patient, to-morrow't shall be mended,
And for this night we'll fast for company. 180
Come I will bring thee to thy bridal chamber.

> [*Exeunt.*

Enter Servants severally.

NATHANIEL

Peter, didst ever see the like?

PETER

He kills her in her own humour.

    Enter Curtis.

GRUMIO

Where is he?

CURTIS

In her chamber,   185

Making a sermon of continency to her;

And rails, and swears, and rates, that she, poor
    soul,

Knows not which way to stand, to look, to speak,

And sits as one new risen from a dream.

Away, away, for he is coming hither. [*Exeunt.* 190

    Enter Petruchio.

PETRUCHIO

Thus have I politicly begun my reign,

And 'tis my hope to end successfully.

My falcon now is sharp, and passing empty,

And till she stoop, she must not be full-gorged,

For then she never looks upon her lure.   195

Another way I have to man my haggard,

To make her come, and know her keeper's call.

That is, to watch her, as we watch these kites,

That bate, and beat, and will not be obedient.

She eat no meat to-day, nor none shall eat.   200

Last night she slept not, nor to-night she shall
    not.

As with the meat, some undeserved fault

I'll find about the making of the bed;

And here I'll fling the pillow, there the bolster,

This way the coverlet, another way the sheets.   205
Ay, and amid this hurly I intend
That all is done in reverent care of her;
And in conclusion, she shall watch all night,
And if she chance to nod, I'll rail and brawl,
And with the clamour keep her still awake.   210
This is a way to kill a wife with kindness,
And thus I'll curb her mad and headstrong hu-
      mour.
He that knows better how to tame a shrew,
Now let him speak, 'tis charity to shew.   [*Exit.*

Scene two

>   *Padua. The Square, before Baptista's*
>   *house. Enter Tranio as Lucentio, and*
>   *Hortensio as Licio.*

  TRANIO

Is't possible friend Licio, that Mistress Bianca
Doth fancy any other but Lucentio?
I tell you sir, she bears me fair in hand.

  HORTENSIO

Sir, to satisfy you in what I have said,
Stand by, and mark the manner of his teaching.   5

>   [*They stand aside.*
>   *Enter Bianca and Lucentio as Cambio.*

  LUCENTIO

Now mistress, profit you in what you read?

  BIANCA

What master read you? First resolve me that.

LUCENTIO

I read that I profess, the Art to Love.

BIANCA

And may you prove sir, master of your art.

LUCENTIO

While you sweet dear prove mistress of my heart.   10

[*They retire.*

HORTENSIO

Quick proceeders marry! Now tell me I pray,
You that durst swear that your mistress Bianca
Loved none in the world so well as Lucentio.

TRANIO

O despiteful love, unconstant womankind!
I tell thee Licio this is wonderful.   15

HORTENSIO

Mistake no more, I am not Licio,
Nor a musician, as I seem to be,
But one that scorn to live in this disguise,
For such a one as leaves a gentleman,
And makes a god of such a cullion.   20
Know sir, that I am called Hortensio.

TRANIO

Signior Hortensio, I have often heard
Of your entire affection to Bianca,
And since mine eyes are witness of her lightness,
I will with you, if you be so contented,   25
Forswear Bianca and her love for ever.

HORTENSIO

See how they kiss and court. Signior Lucentio,
Here is my hand, and here I firmly vow

Never to woo her more, but do forswear her,
As one unworthy all the former favours   30
That I have fondly flattered her withal.

TRANIO

And here I take the like unfeigned oath,
Never to marry with her, though she would
    entreat.
Fie on her! See how beastly she doth court him.

HORTENSIO

Would all the world but he had quite forsworn.   35
For me, that I may surely keep mine oath,
I will be married to a wealthy widow,
Ere three days pass, which hath as long loved me
As I have loved this proud disdainful haggard.
And so farewell Signior Lucentio.   40
Kindness in women, not their beauteous looks,
Shall win my love—and so, I take my leave,
In resolution as I swore before.

> [*Exit Hortensio; Lucentio
>   and Bianca advance.*

TRANIO

Mistress Bianca, bless you with such grace,
As 'longeth to a lover's blessed case.   45
Nay, I have ta'en you napping gentle love,
And have forsworn you, with Hortensio.

BIANCA

Tranio you jest, but have you both forsworn me?

TRANIO

Mistress we have.

LUCENTIO
> Then we are rid of Licio.

TRANIO
I' faith he'll have a lusty widow now,   50
That shall be wooed and wedded in a day.

BIANCA
God give him joy.

TRANIO
Ay, and he'll tame her.

BIANCA
> He says so, Tranio.

TRANIO
Faith he is gone unto the taming school.

BIANCA
The taming school? What, is there such a place?   55

TRANIO
Ay mistress, and Petruchio is the master,
That teacheth tricks eleven and twenty long,
To tame a shrew, and charm her chattering
  tongue.
> *Enter Biondello.*

BIONDELLO
O master, master, I have watched so long,
That I am dog-weary, but at last I spied   60
An ancient angel coming down the hill,
Will serve the turn.

TRANIO
> What is he Biondello?

BIONDELLO
Master, a mercatant, or a pedant,

I know not what, but formal in apparel,
In gait and countenance surly like a father.   65

LUCENTIO

And what of him Tranio?

TRANIO

If he be credulous, and trust my tale,
I'll make him glad to seem Vincentio,
And give assurance to Baptista Minola,
As if he were the right Vincentio.   70
Take in your love, and then let me alone.

          [*Exeunt Lucentio and Bianca.*
     Enter Pedant.

PEDANT

God save you sir.

TRANIO

                    And you sir, you are welcome.
Travel you far on, or are you at the furthest?

PEDANT

Sir, at the furthest for a week or two,
But then up further, and as far as Rome,   ·   75
And so to Tripoli, if God lend me life.

TRANIO

What countryman I pray?

PEDANT

                              Of Mantua.

TRANIO

Of Mantua sir? Marry God forbid!
And come to Padua, careless of your life?

PEDANT

My life sir? How, I pray? For that goes hard.   80

TRANIO

'Tis death for any one in Mantua
To come to Padua—know you not the cause?
Your ships are stayed at Venice, and the Duke,
For private quarrel 'twixt your Duke and him,
Hath published and proclaimed it openly.   85
'Tis marvel, but that you are but newly come,
You might have heard it else proclaimed about.

PEDANT

Alas sir, it is worse for me than so,
For I have bills for money by exchange
From Florence, and must here deliver them.   90

TRANIO

Well sir, to do you courtesy,
This will I do, and this I will advise you—
First tell me, have you ever been at Pisa?

PEDANT

Ay sir, in Pisa have I often been,
Pisa renowned for grave citizens.   95

TRANIO

Among them know you one Vincentio?

PEDANT

I know him not, but I have heard of him.
A merchant of incomparable wealth.

TRANIO

He is my father sir, and sooth to say,
In countenance somewhat doth resemble you.   100

BIONDELLO [*aside*].

As much as an apple doth an oyster, and all one.

TRANIO

To save your life in this extremity,
This favour will I do you for his sake,
And think it not the worst of all your fortunes,
That you are like to Sir Vincentio.   105
His name and credit shall you undertake,
And in my house you shall be friendly lodged.
Look that you take upon you as you should.
You understand me sir—so shall you stay
Till you have done your business in the city.   110
If this be courtesy, sir, accept of it.

PEDANT

O sir I do, and will repute you ever
The patron of my life and liberty.

TRANIO

Then go with me, to make the matter good.
This by the way I let you understand,   115
My father is here looked for every day,
To pass assurance of a dower in marriage
'Twixt me and one Baptista's daughter here.
In all these circumstances I'll instruct you.
Go with me sir, to clothe you as becomes you.   120
                                        [*Exeunt.*

Scene three

> *A room in Petruchio's house.*
> *Enter Katharine and Grumio.*

GRUMIO

No, no forsooth, I dare not for my life.

KATHARINE

The more my wrong, the more his spite appears.
What, did he marry me to famish me?
Beggars that come unto my father's door,
Upon entreaty have a present alms;   5
If not, elsewhere they meet with charity.
But I, who never knew how to entreat,
Nor never needed that I should entreat,
Am starved for meat, giddy for lack of sleep;
With oaths kept waking, and with brawling
    fed;   10
And that which spites me more than all these
    wants,
He does it under name of perfect love;
As who should say, if I should sleep or eat,
'Twere deadly sickness or else present death.
I prithee go, and get me some repast,   15
I care not what, so it be wholesome food.

GRUMIO

What say you to a neat's foot?

KATHARINE

'Tis passing good, I prithee let me have it.

GRUMIO

I fear it is too choleric a meat.
How say you to a fat tripe finely broiled?   20

KATHARINE

I like it well, good Grumio fetch it me.

GRUMIO

I cannot tell, I fear 'tis choleric.
What say you to a piece of beef and mustard?

KATHARINE

A dish that I do love to feed upon.

GRUMIO

Ay, but the mustard is too hot a little.   25

KATHARINE

Why then the beef, and let the mustard rest.

GRUMIO

Nay then I will not, you shall have the mustard,
Or else you get no beef of Grumio.

KATHARINE

Then both, or one, or any thing thou wilt.

GRUMIO

Why then the mustard without the beef.   30

KATHARINE

Go get thee gone, thou false deluding slave,

                                        [*Beats him.*

That feed'st me with the very name of meat.
Sorrow on thee, and all the pack of you
That triumph thus upon my misery.
Go get thee gone, I say.   35

> *Enter Petruchio and Hortensio*
> *with meat.*

PETRUCHIO

How fares my Kate? What sweeting, all amort?

HORTENSIO

Mistress, what cheer?

                    Faith as cold as can be.

PETRUCHIO

Pluck up thy spirits, look cheerfully upon me,

Here love, thou seest how diligent I am,
To dress thy meat myself, and bring it thee: 40
I am sure sweet Kate, this kindness merits
    thanks.
What, not a word? Nay then, thou lov'st it not.
And all my pains is sorted to no proof.
Here, take away this dish.

      KATHARINE

                    I pray you let it stand.

      PETRUCHIO

The poorest service is repaid with thanks,   45
And so shall mine before you touch the meat.

      KATHARINE

I thank you sir.

      HORTENSIO

Signior Petruchio fie, you are to blame.
Come Mistress Kate, I'll bear you company.

      PETRUCHIO [*aside to Hortensio*]

Eat it up all Hortensio, if thou lov'st me.   50
[*To Katharine.*] Much good do it unto thy
    gentle heart.
Kate, eat apace. And now my honey love,
Will we return unto thy father's house,
And revel it as bravely as the best,
With silken coats and caps, and golden rings,   55
With ruffs and cuffs, and farthingales, and things;
With scarfs, and fans, and double change of
    bravery,
With amber bracelets, beads, and all this knav-
    ery.

What hast thou dined? The tailor stays thy lei-
  sure,
To deck thy body with his ruffling treasure.   60
        Enter Tailor.
Come tailor, let us see these ornaments.
Lay forth the gown.
        Enter Haberdasher.
                      What news with you sir?
    HABERDASHER
Here is the cap your worship did bespeak.
    PETRUCHIO
Why this was moulded on a porringer;
A velvet dish. Fie, fie, 'tis lewd and filthy,   65
Why 'tis a cockle or a walnut-shell,
A knack, a toy, a trick, a baby's cap.
Away with it, come, let me have a bigger.
    KATHARINE
I'll have no bigger. This doth fit the time,
And gentlewomen wear such caps as these.   70
    PETRUCHIO
When you are gentle, you shall have one too,
And not till then.
    HORTENSIO [*aside*]
                    That will not be in haste.
    KATHARINE
Why sir I trust I may have leave to speak,
And speak I will. I am no child, no babe;
Your betters have endured me say my mind,   75
And if you cannot, best you stop your ears.
My tongue will tell the anger of my heart,

Or else my heart, concealing it, will break,
And rather than it shall, I will be free
Even to the uttermost as I please in words.   80

KATHARINE — PETRUCHIO

PETRUCHIO

Why thou sayst true, it is a paltry cap,
A custard-coffin, a bauble, a silken pie.
I love thee well in that thou lik'st it not.

KATHARINE

Love me or love me not, I like the cap,
And it I will have, or I will have none.   85

PETRUCHIO

Thy gown? Why ay—come tailor let us see't.
O mercy God, what masking stuff is here?
What's this? A sleeve? 'Tis like a demi-cannon.
What, up and down carved like an apple tart?
Here's snip, and nip, and cut, and slish and slash,   90
Like to a censer in a barber's shop.
Why what a devil's name, tailor, call'st thou this?

HORTENSIO [*aside*]

I see she's like to have neither cap nor gown.

TAILOR

You bid me make it orderly and well,
According to the fashion, and the time.   95

PETRUCHIO

Marry and did. But if you be remembered,
I did not bid you mar it to the time.
Go hop me over every kennel home,
For you shall hop without my custom sir.
I'll none of it. Hence, make your best of it.   100

KATHARINE

I never saw a better-fashioned gown,
More quaint, more pleasing, nor more com-
mendable.
Belike you mean to make a puppet of me.

PETRUCHIO

Why true, he means to make a puppet of thee.

TAILOR

She says your worship means to make a puppet   105
of her.

PETRUCHIO

O monstrous arrogance! Thou liest, thou thread,
thou thimble,
Thou yard, three-quarters, half-yard, quarter,
nail,
Thou flea, thou nit, thou winter-cricket thou!   110
Braved in mine own house with a skein of
thread?
Away thou rag, thou quantity, thou remnant,
Or I shall so be-mete thee with thy yard,
As thou shalt think on prating whilst thou livest.
I tell thee I, that thou hast marred her gown.   115

TAILOR

Your worship is deceived, the gown is made
Just as my master had direction.
Grumio gave order how it should be done.

GRUMIO

I gave him no order; I gave him the stuff.

TAILOR

But how did you desire it should be made?   120

GRUMIO

Marry sir with needle and thread.

TAILOR

But did you not request to have it cut?

GRUMIO

Thou hast faced many things.

TAILOR

I have.

GRUMIO

Face not me. Thou hast braved many men, brave 125
not me; I will neither be faced nor braved. I say
unto thee, I bid thy master cut out the gown, but
I did not bid him cut it to pieces. Ergo, thou
liest.

TAILOR

Why here is the note of the fashion to testify. 130

PETRUCHIO

Read it.

GRUMIO

The note lies in's throat if he say I said so.

TAILOR [*reads*]

Imprimis, a loose-bodied gown— 135

GRUMIO

Master, if ever I said loose-bodied gown, sew me
in the skirts of it, and beat me to death with a
bottom of brown thread. I said a gown.

PETRUCHIO

Proceed.

TAILOR

With a small compassed cape. 140

GRUMIO

I confess the cape.

TAILOR

With a trunk sleeve.

GRUMIO

I confess two sleeves.

TAILOR

The sleeves curiously cut.

PETRUCHIO

Ay there's the villainy.   145

GRUMIO

Error i' th' bill sir, error i' th' bill. I commanded
the sleeves should be cut out, and sewed up
again, and that I'll prove upon thee, though thy
little finger be armed in a thimble.

TAILOR

This is true that I say, an I had thee in place   150
where, thou shouldst know it.

GRUMIO

I am for thee straight. Take thou the bill, give me
thy mete-yard, and spare not me.

HORTENSIO

God-a-mercy Grumio, then he shall have no
odds.   155

PETRUCHIO

Well sir, in brief, the gown is not for me.

GRUMIO

You are i' th' right sir, 'tis for my mistress.

PETRUCHIO

Go take it up unto thy master's use.

GRUMIO

Villain, not for thy life. Take up my mistress' 160
gown for thy master's use!

PETRUCHIO

Why sir, what's your conceit in that?

GRUMIO

O sir, the conceit is deeper than you think for.
Take up my mistress' gown to his master's use!
O fie, fie, fie! 165

PETRUCHIO [*aside to Hortensio*].

Hortensio, say thou wilt see the tailor paid.
[*To Tailor*.] Go take it hence; be gone, and say
no more.

HORTENSIO

Tailor, I'll pay thee for thy gown to-morrow.
Take no unkindness of his hasty words.
Away, I say, commend me to thy master. 170

[*Exeunt Tailor and Haberdasher*.

PETRUCHIO

Well, come my Kate, we will unto your father's,
Even in these honest mean habiliments.
Our purses shall be proud, our garments poor;
For 'tis the mind that makes the body rich.
And as the sun breaks through the darkest
clouds, 175
So honour peereth in the meanest habit.
What, is the jay more precious than the lark,
Because his feathers are more beautiful?
Or is the adder better than the eel,
Because his painted skin contents the eye? 180

O no good Kate, neither art thou the worse
For this poor furniture and mean array.
If thou account'st it shame, lay it on me,
And therefore frolic; we will hence forthwith,
To feast and sport us at thy father's house.   185
Go call my men, and let us straight to him,
And bring our horses unto Long-lane end.
There will we mount, and thither walk on foot.
Let's see, I think 'tis now some seven o'clock,
And well we may come there by dinner-time.   190

    KATHARINE

I dare assure you sir, 'tis almost two,
And 'twill be supper-time ere you come there.

    PETRUCHIO

It shall be seven ere I go to horse.
Look what I speak, or do, or think to do,
You are still crossing it. Sirs let't alone,   195
I will not go to-day, and ere I do,
It shall be what o'clock I say it is.

    HORTENSIO

Why so this gallant will command the sun.

                [*Exeunt.*

Scene four

    *Padua. The Square, before Baptista's
    house. Enter Tranio, and the Pedant
    dressed like Vincentio.*

    TRANIO

Sir, this is the house, please it you that I call?

PEDANT

Ay what else? And but I be deceived,
Signior Baptista may remember me,
Near twenty years ago in Genoa,
Where we were lodgers at the Pegasus. 5

TRANIO

'Tis well, and hold your own in any case,
With such austerity as 'longeth to a father.
Enter Biondello.

PEDANT

I warrant you. But sir, here comes your boy,
'Twere good he were schooled.

TRANIO

Fear you not him. Sirrah Biondello, 10
Now do your duty throughly, I advise you.
Imagine 'twere the right Vincentio.

BIONDELLO

Tut, fear not me.

TRANIO

But hast thou done thy errand to Baptista?

BIONDELLO

I told him that your father was at Venice, 15
And that you looked for him this day in Padua.

TRANIO

Thou'rt a tall fellow, hold thee that to drink.
Enter Baptista and Lucentio as Cambio.
Here comes Baptista—set your countenance sir.
Signior Baptista, you are happily met.
[*To the Pedant.*] Sir, this is the gentleman I told
you of. 20

I pray you stand good father to me now,
Give me Bianca for my patrimony.

PEDANT

Soft son.
Sir by your leave, having come to Padua
To gather in some debts, my son Lucentio   25
Made me acquainted with a weighty cause
Of love between your daughter and himself.
And, for the good report I hear of you,
And for the love he beareth to your daughter,
And she to him, to stay him not too long,   30
I am content, in a good father's care,
To have him matched, and if you please to like
No worse than I, upon some agreement
Me shall you find ready and willing
With one consent to have her so bestowed.   35
For curious I cannot be with you,
Signior Baptista, of whom I hear so well.

BAPTISTA

Sir, pardon me in what I have to say;
Your plainness and your shortness please me
     well.
Right true it is your son Lucentio here   40
Doth love my daughter, and she loveth him,
Or both dissemble deeply their affections.
And therefore if you say no more than this,
That like a father you will deal with him,
And pass my daughter a sufficient dower,   45
The match is made, and all is done:
Your son shall have my daughter with consent.

TRANIO

I thank you sir. Where then do you hold best
We be affied and such assurance ta'en,
As shall with either part's agreement stand?   50

BAPTISTA

Not in my house Lucentio, for you know
Pitchers have ears, and I have many servants;
Besides, old Gremio is hearkening still,
And happily we might be interrupted.

TRANIO

Then at my lodging, an it like you.   55
There doth my father lie; and there this night
We'll pass the business privately and well.
Send for your daughter by your servant here,
My boy shall fetch the scrivener presently.
The worst is this, that at so slender warning,   60
You are like to have a thin and slender pittance.

BAPTISTA

It likes me well. Cambio, hie you home,
And bid Bianca make her ready straight;
And if you will tell what hath happened,
Lucentio's father is arrived in Padua,   65
And how she's like to be Lucentio's wife.

BIONDELLO

I pray the gods she may with all my heart.

TRANIO

Dally not with the gods, but get thee gone.

                              [*Exit Biondello.*

Signior Baptista, shall I lead the way?
Welcome, one mess is like to be your cheer.   70

Come sir, we will better it in Pisa.

BAPTISTA

I follow you.

> [*Exeunt Tranio, Pedant, and Baptista.
> Enter Biondello.*

BIONDELLO

Cambio—

LUCENTIO

What sayst thou Biondello?

BIONDELLO

You saw my master wink and laugh upon you?   75

LUCENTIO

Biondello, what of that?

BIONDELLO

Faith nothing, but has left me here behind to
expound the meaning or moral of his signs and
tokens.   80

LUCENTIO

I pray thee moralize them.

BIONDELLO

Then thus. Baptista is safe talking with the de-
ceiving father of a deceitful son.

LUCENTIO

And what of him?

BIONDELLO

His daughter is to be brought by you to the   85
supper.

LUCENTIO

And then?

BIONDELLO

The old priest at Saint Luke's church is at your
command at all hours.

LUCENTIO

And what of all this?   90

BIONDELLO

I cannot tell, except they are busied about a
counterfeit assurance. Take you assurance of
her, cum privilegio ad imprimendum solum, to
th' church—take the priest, clerk, and some sufficient honest witnesses: 95

If this be not that you look for, I have no more
    to say,

But bid Bianca farewell for ever and a day.

                                    [*Going.*

LUCENTIO

Hear'st thou Biondello?

BIONDELLO

I cannot tarry. I knew a wench married in an
afternoon as she went to the garden for parsley   100
to stuff a rabbit, and so may you sir. And so
adieu sir. My master hath appointed me to go to
Saint Luke's, to bid the priest be ready to come
against you come with your appendix.   [*Exit.*   105

LUCENTIO

I may and will, if she be so contented.

She will be pleased, then wherefore should I
    doubt?

Hap what hap may, I'll roundly go about her.

It shall go hard if Cambio go without her. [*Exit.*

Scene five

The highway to Padua. Enter Petruchio,
Katharine, Hortensio, and Servants.

PETRUCHIO

Come on a God's name, once more toward our
  father's.
Good lord how bright and goodly shines the
  moon!

KATHARINE

The moon? The sun. It is not moonlight now.

PETRUCHIO

I say it is the moon that shines so bright.

KATHARINE

I know it is the sun that shines so bright.   5

PETRUCHIO

Now by my mother's son, and that's myself,
It shall be moon, or star, or what I list,
Or e'er I journey to your father's house.
Go on, and fetch our horses back again.
Evermore crossed and crossed, nothing but
  crossed!   10

HORTENSIO [*aside to Katharine*]

Say as he says, or we shall never go.

KATHARINE

Forward I pray, since we have come so far,
And be it moon, or sun, or what you please.
An if you please to call it a rush-candle,
Henceforth I vow it shall be so for me.   15

PETRUCHIO
I say it is the moon.

KATHARINE
                    I know it is the moon.

PETRUCHIO
Nay then you lie. It is the blessed sun.

KATHARINE
Then God be blessed, it is the blessed sun,
But sun it is not, when you say it is not,
And the moon changes even as your mind.   20
What you will have it named, even that it is,
And so it shall be still for Katharine.

HORTENSIO [*aside*]
Petruchio, go thy ways, the field is won.

PETRUCHIO
Well, forward, forward, thus the bowl should
    run,
And not unluckily against the bias.   25

Enter Vincentio.

But soft, company is coming here.
[*To Vincentio.*] Good morrow gentle mistress,
    where away?
Tell me sweet Kate, and tell me truly too,
Hast thou beheld a fresher gentlewoman?
Such war of white and red within her cheeks!   30
What stars do spangle heaven with such beauty,
As those two eyes become that heavenly face?
Fair lovely maid, once more good day to thee.
Sweet Kate embrace her for her beauty's sake.

HORTENSIO [*aside*]

'A will make the man mad, to make a woman of   35
him.

KATHARINE

Young budding virgin, fair, and fresh, and sweet,
Whither away, or where is thy abode?
Happy the parents of so fair a child;
Happier the man whom favourable stars   40
Allots thee for his lovely bedfellow.

PETRUCHIO

Why how now Kate, I hope thou art not mad.
This is a man, old, wrinkled, faded, withered,
And not a maiden, as thou sayst he is.

KATHARINE

Pardon old father my mistaking eyes,   45
That have been so bedazzled with the sun,
That every thing I look on seemeth green.
Now I perceive thou art a reverend father.
Pardon I pray thee, for my mad mistaking.

PETRUCHIO

Do good old grandsire, and withal make known   50
Which way thou travellest; if along with us,
We shall be joyful of thy company.

VINCENTIO

Fair sir, and you my merry mistress,
That with your strange encounter much amazed
me,
My name is called Vincentio, my dwelling Pisa,   55
And bound I am to Padua, there to visit
A son of mine, which long I have not seen.

PETRUCHIO
What is his name?
VINCENTIO
                    Lucentio gentle sir.
PETRUCHIO
Happily met, the happier for thy son.
And now by law, as well as reverend age,   60
I may entitle thee my loving father.
The sister to my wife, this gentlewoman,
Thy son by this hath married. Wonder not,
Nor be not grieved; she is of good esteem,
Her dowry wealthy, and of worthy birth;   65
Beside, so qualified, as may beseem
The spouse of any noble gentleman.
Let me embrace with old Vincentio,
And wander we to see thy honest son,
Who will of thy arrival be full joyous.   70
VINCENTIO
But is this true, or is it else your pleasure,
Like pleasant travellers to break a jest
Upon the company you overtake?
HORTENSIO
I do assure thee father, so it is.
PETRUCHIO
Come go along and see the truth hereof,   ·   75
For our first merriment hath made thee jealous.
                    [*Exeunt Petruchio, Katharine,*
                         Vincentio and Servants.
HORTENSIO
Well Petruchio, this has put me in heart.

Have to my widow, and if she be froward,
Then hast thou taught Hortensio to be untoward.
                                        [*Exit.*

Act five Scene one

> *Padua. The Square, before Lucentio's
> house. Enter Gremio. Then enter Bion-
> dello, Lucentio and Bianca.*

BIONDELLO

Softly and swiftly sir, for the priest is ready.

LUCENTIO

I fly Biondello; but they may chance to need thee
at home, therefore leave us.

BIONDELLO

Nay faith, I'll see the church o' your back, and   5
then come back to my master as soon as I can.
          [*Exeunt Lucentio, Bianca, and Biondello.*

GREMIO

I marvel Cambio comes not all this while.
          *Enter Petruchio, Katharine, Vincentio,
          Grumio, and Servants.*

PETRUCHIO

Sir, here's the door, this is Lucentio's house.
My father's bears more toward the market place.   10
Thither must I, and here I leave you sir.

VINCENTIO

You shall not choose but drink before you go.
I think I shall command your welcome here,

And by all likelihood some cheer is toward.

[Knocks.

GREMIO

They're busy within; you were best knock
  louder.   15

Enter Pedant above.

PEDANT

What's he that knocks as he would beat down
the gate?

VINCENTIO

Is Signior Lucentio within sir?

PEDANT

He's within sir, but not to be spoken withal.   20

VINCENTIO

What if a man bring him a hundred pound or
two to make merry withal?

PEDANT

Keep your hundred pounds to yourself, he shall
need none so long as I live.   25

PETRUCHIO

Nay, I told you your son was well beloved in
Padua. Do you hear sir? To leave frivolous
circumstances, I pray you tell Signior Lucentio
that his father is come from Pisa, and is here at
the door to speak with him.   30

PEDANT

Thou liest. His father is come from Mantua, and
here looking out at the window.

VINCENTIO

Art thou his father?

PEDANT

Ay sir, so his mother says, if I may believe her.   35

PETRUCHIO [*to Vincentio*]

Why how now gentleman! Why this is flat knavery to take upon you another man's name.

PEDANT

Lay hands on the villain. I believe 'a means to
cozen somebody in this city under my counte-   40
nance.

Enter Biondello.

BIONDELLO

I have seen them in the church together. God
send 'em good shipping. But who is here? Mine
old master Vincentio! Now we are undone, and
brought to nothing.   45

VINCENTIO

Come hither crack-hemp.

BIONDELLO

I hope I may choose sir.

VINCENTIO

Come hither you rogue. What, have you forgot
me?   50

BIONDELLO

Forgot you? No sir. I could not forget you, for I
never saw you before in all my life.

VINCENTIO

What, you notorious villain, didst thou never see
thy master's father, Vincentio?   55

BIONDELLO

What, my old worshipful old master? Yes, marry sir, see where he looks out of the window.

VINCENTIO

Is't so indeed?   [*Beats Biondello.*

BIONDELLO

Help, help, help, here's a madman will murder   60
me!   [*Exit.*

PEDANT

Help son, help, Signior Baptista!

PETRUCHIO

Prithee Kate, let's stand aside and see the end of
this controversy.   [*They retire.*
    Enter Pedant below; Baptista, Tranio,
    and Servants.

TRANIO

Sir, what are you that offer to beat my servant?   65

VINCENTIO

What am I sir? Nay, what are you sir? O im-
mortal gods! O fine villain! A silken doublet, a
velvet hose, a scarlet cloak, and a copatain hat!
O I am undone, I am undone! While I play the   70
good husband at home, my son and my servant
spend all at the university.

TRANIO

How now, what's the matter?

BAPTISTA

What, is the man lunatic?

TRANIO

Sir, you seem a sober ancient gentleman by your   75
habit. But your words show you a madman. Why
sir, what 'cerns it you if I wear pearl and gold?

I thank my good father, I am able to maintain it.

VINCENTIO

Thy father? O villain, he is a sail-maker in Bergamo. 80

BAPTISTA

You mistake sir, you mistake sir. Pray what do you think is his name?

VINCENTIO

His name? As if I knew not his name. I have brought him up ever since he was three years old, 85 and his name is Tranio.

PEDANT

Away, away, mad ass! His name is Lucentio, and he is mine only son, and heir to the lands of me, Signior Vincentio.

VINCENTIO

Lucentio? O he hath murdered his master. Lay 90 hold on him, I charge you, in the Duke's name. O my son, my son! Tell me thou villain, where is my son Lucentio?

TRANIO

Call forth an officer.

Enter Servant with Officer.

Carry this mad knave to the gaol. Father Bap- 95 tista, I charge you see that he be forthcoming.

VINCENTIO

Carry me to the gaol?

GREMIO

Stay officer, he shall not go to prison.

BAPTISTA

Talk not Signior Gremio. I say he shall go to
prison.   100

GREMIO

Take heed Signior Baptista, lest you be cony-
catched in this business. I dare swear this is the
right Vincentio.

PEDANT

Swear if thou darest.

GREMIO

Nay, I dare not swear it.   105

TRANIO

Then thou wert best say that I am not Lucentio.

GREMIO

Yes, I know thee to be Signior Lucentio.

BAPTISTA

Away with the dotard, to the gaol with him!   110

VINCENTIO

Thus strangers may be haled and abused.
O monstrous villainy!

> *Enter Biondello, with Lucentio and*
> *Bianca.*

BIONDELLO

O we are spoiled, and yonder he is. Deny him,
forswear him, or else we are all undone.

LUCENTIO

Pardon sweet father.   [*Kneels.*

VINCENTIO

> Lives my sweet son?   115
> [*Exeunt Biondello, Tranio, and Pedant.*

BIANCA
Pardon dear father.   [*Kneels.*

BAPTISTA
                How hast thou offended?
Where is Lucentio?

LUCENTIO
                Here's Lucentio,
Right son unto the right Vincentio,
That have by marriage made thy daughter
    mine,
While counterfeit supposes bleared thine eyne.   120

GREMIO
Here's packing, with a witness, to deceive us all!

VINCENTIO
Where is that damned villain Tranio,
That faced and braved me in this matter so?

BAPTISTA
Why tell me, is not this my Cambio?   125

BIANCA
Cambio is changed into Lucentio.

LUCENTIO
Love wrought these miracles. Bianca's love
Made me exchange my state with Tranio,
While he did bear my countenance in the town,
And happily I have arrived at last   130
Unto the wished haven of my bliss.
What Tranio did, myself enforced him to;
Then pardon him sweet father, for my sake.

VINCENTIO

I'll slit the villain's nose that would have sent me
to the gaol.   135

BAPTISTA [*to Lucentio*]

But do you hear sir? Have you married my
daughter without asking my good will?

VINCENTIO

Fear not Baptista, we will content you, go to.
But I will in to be revenged for this villainy.   140

[*Exit*.

BAPTISTA

And I, to sound the depth of this knavery. [*Exit*.

LUCENTIO

Look not pale Bianca, thy father will not frown.

[*Exeunt Lucentio and Bianca*.

GREMIO

My cake is dough, but I'll in among the rest;   145
Out of hope of all, but my share of the feast.

[*Exit*.

Petruchio and Katharine come forward.

KATHARINE

Husband let's follow, to see the end of this ado.

PETRUCHIO

First kiss me Kate, and we will.

KATHARINE

What, in the midst of the street?

PETRUCHIO

What art thou ashamed of me?   150

KATHARINE

No sir, God forbid, but ashamed to kiss.

PETRUCHIO

Why then let's home again. Come sirrah, let's
    away.

KATHARINE

Nay, I will give thee a kiss [*kisses him*]; now
    pray thee love, stay.

PETRUCHIO

Is not this well? Come my sweet Kate.
Better once than never, for never too late.   155

[*Exeunt.*

Scene two

> A room in Lucentio's house. Enter Bap-
> tista, Vincentio, Gremio, Pedant, Lucen-
> tio, Bianca, Petruchio, Katharine, Hor-
> tensio and Widow, Biondello and Gru-
> mio; Tranio with Servants bringing in a
> banquet.

LUCENTIO

At last, though long, our jarring notes agree,
And time it is, when raging war is done,
To smile at 'scapes and perils overblown.
My fair Bianca, bid my father welcome,
While I with selfsame kindness welcome thine.   5
Brother Petruchio, sister Katharina,
And thou Hortensio, with thy loving widow,
Feast with the best, and welcome to my house.

My banquet is to close our stomachs up
After our great good cheer. Pray you sit down, 10
For now we sit to chat, as well as eat. [*They sit.*

PETRUCHIO
Nothing but sit and sit, and eat and eat!

BAPTISTA
Padua affords this kindness, son Petruchio.

PETRUCHIO
Padua affords nothing but what is kind.

HORTENSIO
For both our sakes I would that word were true. 15

PETRUCHIO
Now for my life, Hortensio fears his widow.

WIDOW
Then never trust me if I be afeard.

PETRUCHIO
You are very sensible, and yet you miss my
sense;
I mean Hortensio is afeard of you.

WIDOW
He that is giddy thinks the world turns round. 20

PETRUCHIO
Roundly replied.

KATHARINE
Mistress, how mean you that?

WIDOW
Thus I conceive by him.

PETRUCHIO
Conceives by me? How likes Hortensio that?

HORTENSIO

My widow says, thus she conceives her tale.

PETRUCHIO

Very well mended. Kiss him for that good
    widow. 25

KATHARINE

He that is giddy thinks the world turns round—
I pray you tell me what you meant by that.

WIDOW

Your husband, being troubled with a shrew,
Measures my husband's sorrow by his woe—
And now you know my meaning. 30

KATHARINE

A very mean meaning.

WIDOW

                  Right, I mean you.

KATHARINE

And I am mean indeed, respecting you.

PETRUCHIO

To her Kate!

HORTENSIO

To her widow!

PETRUCHIO

A hundred marks, my Kate does put her down. 35

HORTENSIO

That's my office.

PETRUCHIO

Spoke like an officer—ha' to thee lad.

                [*Drinks to Hortensio.*

BAPTISTA

How likes Gremio these quick-witted folks?

GREMIO

Believe me sir, they butt together well.

BIANCA

Head and butt—an hasty-witted body   40
Would say your head and butt were head and
   horn.

VINCENTIO

Ay mistress bride, hath that awakened you?

BIANCA

Ay, but not frighted me, therefore I'll sleep
   again.

PETRUCHIO

Nay that you shall not; since you have begun,
Have at you for a bitter jest or two.   45

BIANCA

Am I your bird? I mean to shift my bush,
And then pursue me as you draw your bow.
You are welcome all.

   [*Exeunt Bianca, Katharine, and Widow.*

PETRUCHIO

She hath prevented me. Here Signior Tranio,
This bird you aimed at, though you hit her not.   50
Therefore a health to all that shot and missed.

TRANIO

O sir, Lucentio slipped me like his greyhound,
Which runs himself, and catches for his master.

PETRUCHIO

A good swift simile, but something currish.

TRANIO

'Tis well sir, that you hunted for yourself.   55

'Tis thought your deer does hold you at a bay.

BAPTISTA

O, o, Petruchio! Tranio hits you now.

LUCENTIO

I thank thee for that gird good Tranio.

HORTENSIO

Confess, confess, hath he not hit you here?

PETRUCHIO

'A has a little galled me I confess;   60

And as the jest did glance away from me,

'Tis ten to one it maimed you two outright.

BAPTISTA

Now in good sadness son Petruchio,

I think thou hast the veriest shrew of all.

PETRUCHIO

Well, I say no. And therefore, for assurance,   65

Let's each one send unto his wife,

And he whose wife is most obedient,

To come at first when he doth send for her,

Shall win the wager which we will propose.

HORTENSIO

Content—what's the wager?

LUCENTIO

                              Twenty crowns.   70

PETRUCHIO

Twenty crowns?

I'll venture so much of my hawk or hound,

But twenty times so much upon my wife.

LUCENTIO
A hundred then.

HORTENSIO
Content.

PETRUCHIO
A match, 'tis done.

HORTENSIO
Who shall begin?

LUCENTIO
That will I.   75
Go Biondello, bid your mistress come to me.

BIONDELLO
I go.   [*Exit.*

BAPTISTA
Son, I'll be your half, Bianca comes.

LUCENTIO
I'll have no halves. I'll bear it all myself.
Enter Biondello.
How now, what news?

BIONDELLO
Sir, my mistress sends you word   80
That she is busy, and she cannot come.

PETRUCHIO
How? She's busy, and she cannot come?
Is that an answer?

GREMIO
Ay, and a kind one too.
Pray God sir, your wife send you not a worse.

PETRUCHIO
I hope better.   85

HORTENSIO

Sirrah Biondello, go and entreat my wife
To come to me forthwith.   [*Exit Biondello.*

PETRUCHIO

O ho, entreat her!
Nay then she must needs come.

HORTENSIO

I am afraid sir,
Do what you can, yours will not be entreated.
Enter Biondello.
Now, where's my wife?   90

BIONDELLO

She says you have some goodly jest in hand,
She will not come. She bids you come to her.

PETRUCHIO

Worse and worse, she will not come! O vile.
Intolerable, not to be endured!
Sirrah Grumio, go to your mistress;   95
Say I command her come to me. [*Exit Grumio.*

HORTENSIO

I know her answer.

PETRUCHIO

What?

HORTENSIO

She will not.

PETRUCHIO

The fouler fortune mine, and there an end.
Enter Katharine.

BAPTISTA

Now by my holidame here comes Katharina.

KATHARINE

What is your will sir, that you send for me?   100

PETRUCHIO

Where is your sister, and Hortensio's wife?

KATHARINE

They sit conferring by the parlour fire.

PETRUCHIO

Go fetch them hither. If they deny to come,
Swinge me them soundly forth unto their
    husbands.
Away I say, and bring them hither straight.   105

> [*Exit Katharine.*

LUCENTIO

Here is a wonder, if you talk of a wonder.

HORTENSIO

And so it is. I wonder what it bodes.

PETRUCHIO

Marry peace it bodes, and love, and quiet life,
An awful rule, and right supremacy;
And to be short, what not that's sweet and
    happy.   110

BAPTISTA

Now fair befall thee good Petruchio.
The wager thou hast won, and I will add
Unto their losses twenty thousand crowns;
Another dowry to another daughter,
For she is changed, as she had never been.   115

PETRUCHIO

Nay, I will win my wager better yet,
And show more sign of her obedience,

Her new-built virtue and obedience.

>   *Enter Katharine, with Bianca and*
>   *Widow.*

See where she comes, and brings your froward
    wives
As prisoners to her womanly persuasion.   120
Katharine, that cap of yours becomes you not.
Off with that bauble, throw it under foot.

>   [*She obeys.*

WIDOW

Lord, let me never have a cause to sigh,
Till I be brought to such a silly pass.

BIANCA

Fie, what a foolish duty call you this?   125

LUCENTIO

I would your duty were as foolish too.
The wisdom of your duty fair Bianca,
Hath cost me a hundred crowns since supper-
    time.

BIANCA

The more fool you for laying on my duty.

PETRUCHIO

Katharine I charge thee, tell these headstrong
    women,   130
What duty they do owe their lords and husbands.

WIDOW

Come, come, you're mocking; we will have no
    telling.

PETRUCHIO

Come on I say, and first begin with her.

WIDOW

She shall not.

PETRUCHIO

I say she shall—and first begin with her. 135

KATHARINE

Fie, fie, unknit that threatening unkind brow,
And dart not scornful glances from those eyes,
To wound thy lord, thy king, thy governor.
It blots thy beauty, as frosts do bite the meads,
Confounds thy fame, as whirlwinds shake fair
    buds, 140
And in no sense is meet or amiable.
A woman moved, is like a fountain troubled,
Muddy, ill-seeming, thick, bereft of beauty,
And while it is so, none so dry or thirsty
Will deign to sip, or touch one drop of it. 145
Thy husband is thy lord, thy life, thy keeper,
Thy head, thy sovereign; one that cares for thee,
And for thy maintenance; commits his body
To painful labour both by sea and land;
To watch the night in storms, the day in cold, 150
Whilst thou liest warm at home, secure and safe;
And craves no other tribute at thy hands
But love, fair looks, and true obedience—
Too little payment for so great a debt.
Such duty as the subject owes the prince, 155
Even such a woman oweth to her husband;
And when she is froward, peevish, sullen, sour,
And not obedient to his honest will,
What is she but a foul contending rebel,

And graceless traitor to her loving lord?   160
I am ashamed that women are so simple
To offer war, where they should kneel for peace;
Or seek for rule, supremacy, and sway,
When they are bound to serve, love, and obey.
Why are our bodies soft, and weak, and smooth,   165
Unapt to toil and trouble in the world,
But that our soft conditions, and our hearts,
Should well agree with our external parts?
Come, come, you froward and unable worms,
My mind hath been as big as one of yours,   170
My heart as great, my reason haply more,
To bandy word for word, and frown for frown.
But now I see our lances are but straws;
Our strength as weak, our weakness past com-
    pare,
That seeming to be most, which we indeed least
    are.   175
Then vail your stomachs, for it is no boot,
And place your hands below your husband's
    foot.
In token of which duty, if he please,
My hand is ready, may it do him ease.

PETRUCHIO

Why there's a wench! Come on, and kiss me
    Kate.   180

LUCENTIO

Well go thy ways old lad, for thou shalt ha't.

VINCENTIO

'Tis a good hearing, when children are toward.

LUCENTIO

But a harsh hearing, when women are froward.

PETRUCHIO

Come Kate, we'll to bed.

We three are married, but you two are sped. 165

[*To Lucentio.*] 'Twas I won the wager, though
you hit the white.

And being a winner, God give you good night.

[*Exeunt Petruchio and Katharine.*

HORTENSIO

Now go thy ways, thou hast tamed a curst shrow.

LUCENTIO

'Tis a wonder, by your leave, she will be tamed
so. [*Exeunt.*

Shakespeare and His Theatre

BY FRANCIS FERGUSSON

I. SHAKESPEARE'S CAREER

William Shakespeare was christened in Stratford on April twenty-sixth, 1564. The exact date of his birth is unknown, but it is traditionally celebrated on the twenty-third, because that is Saint George's Day, and Saint George is England's patron saint.

The Shakespeares were a prosperous and locally prominent family. William was the oldest of six children. His father, John Shakespeare, the son of a tenant farmer, had moved to Stratford as a young man, and there built for himself a successful business career as a glover and a dealer in wool, timber, and other commodities. John also held office as Justice of the Peace and High Bailiff (Mayor); and late in life he was granted a coat of arms, which made him a "gentleman." Shakespeare's mother, Mary Arden, a member of a family of small landowners, must have brought her husband both social standing and land.

Stratford, about a hundred miles northwest of London, was a prosperous market town, one of the largest in Warwickshire. A great deal is known about Stratford, which enables us to understand something of Shakespeare's boyhood there. The town supported a grammar school which was free to the sons of Burgesses, of whom Shakespeare was one. Grammar schools were designed to prepare their students for one of the universities, and in Stratford the masters were university graduates. The education they gave was narrow but thorough. It included some history and religious instruction, but was based chiefly on Latin and the arts of language: grammar, logic, rhetoric, and what we call "public speaking." Shakespeare read a number of Latin authors, including Ovid and probably Plautus, whose comedies he imitated when he started to write for the stage. The children went to school on weekdays, summer and winter, from seven in the morning until five in the afternoon, with two hours off for dinner. Shakespeare must have started this strict routine as soon as he knew his catechism.

During his boyhood Stratford was regularly visited by touring players, including the best companies in England. The plays they brought were moralizing works on Biblical or classical themes, very wooden compared with what Shakespeare himself would write. But his future profession was highly esteemed; the players were received in the Guildhall by leading citizens, including no doubt Shakespeare's father. For the rest, we may safely imagine Shakespeare as engaged in the usual activities of a boy in a country town, acquiring the intimate knowledge of the countryside and its rural types which is reflected in his plays.

We do not know what Shakespeare did between the time he left school and his departure for London. Some of the stories about him—that he was for a time a country schoolmaster, that he got into trouble for poaching deer—are possible, but unproved. We do know that he married Ann Hathaway, daughter of a yeoman farmer, in 1582, when he was eighteen and she was twenty-three. Their first child, Susan, was baptized six months later. Perhaps the Shakespeares were "betrothed"—which, by the custom of the time, would have made them legally married—some months before the recorded church ceremony. They had two more children, the twins Hamnet and Judith, who were christened in 1585. Shakespeare departed for London very soon after that. He did not take his family with him, for he occupied bachelor's lodgings in London for most of the rest of his life. But he was also a householder in Stratford, and apparently continued to think of himself as a resident.

London, when Shakespeare went there as a young man, in about 1586, was enjoying the great years of Queen Elizabeth's reign. She had ascended the throne in 1558; in 1588 her navy had its famous victory over the Spanish Armada, which marked England's emergence as a great sea-power, and symbolized the national rebirth. The City of London had its ancient mercantile traditions, its bourgeois freedoms, and, among the City officials, a certain Puritanical spirit of its own. But the City had spread far beyond the medieval walls, and Renaissance London contained between 100,000 and 200,000 inhabitants. As the seat of Elizabeth's court it was the unrivaled center of English politics and culture. It was a university town, for the Inns of Court, resident law-schools for young gentlemen of wealth, were there; and it was full of foreigners from the continent of Europe. As a great port it was in touch with the Indies, the Mediterranean, and the Americas. Shakespeare never went to a university, but London was admirably fitted to complete his education in Italian and French, in history and literature, in the great professions, and to give him direct experience of the ways of men at an exciting moment in history. The theatre was near the center of life in Renaissance London, and Shakespeare must have been close to many of the great figures and great events of his time.

Much is known about London and about the theatres where Shakespeare worked, but little is known directly about his own doings. Contemporary comments on him, and on his plays, suggest that most of his great vitality went straight into his work for the theatre. Legal and business documents, church records, and the like, enable the experts to fix a few important dates in his personal and professional life. And the dates of his plays, though disputed in detail, are well enough established to give us the approximate sequence. It is chiefly through a study of his plays in the order in which he wrote them, and in relation to the known facts of his life, that we can gain some understanding of his development. It is convenient (following Professor Peter Alexander and others) to distinguish four main periods in Shakespeare's career:

1. Apprenticeship to the London Theatre: from Shakespeare's arrival in London (circa 1586) until he joined The Lord Chamberlain's Men, in 1594.

Shakespeare entered the theatre as an actor when he first

went to London, or as soon thereafter as he had acquired the necessary training. He was to be an actor and actor-manager for the rest of his life, and in that capacity, rather than as a playwright, he made a very good living. Playwrights received a smaller share of the theatre's revenue then than they do now. They sold their scripts outright, for very small sums, to the actors, who then divided the receipts among themselves. Shakespeare, however, began to write at once. By 1594 he had completed the following list: *Titus Andronicus; Henry VI,* Parts 1, 2, and 3; *The Comedy of Errors; Two Gentlemen of Verona; The Taming of the Shrew; Richard III; Love's Labor's Lost;* and probably *King John.*

Shakespeare's earliest work shows that he began his professional career in the most natural way: by mastering several kinds of plays that were then popular. *The Comedy of Errors, Two Gentlemen of Verona,* and *The Taming of the Shrew* are farces, based on the Latin comedy of Plautus. They have little of the poetry and subtlety of his later and more original comedies, but they are still, as they were when he wrote them, sure and effective popular entertainment. *Titus Andronicus,* a "Senecan" melodrama like other pseudo-classical plays of the time, was successful then, but usually proves too sensational and pompous for the modern stage.

The three parts of *Henry VI* are the first of Shakespeare's "Histories." The history play was a popular and characteristic form in the London theatre as Shakespeare found it. It was taken from one of the widely read Chronicles of English history, like those of Shakespeare's favorite Holinshed—a dramatization of some exciting sequence from the epic struggle of the Crown against the great nobles, the intriguing churchmen, and France and Spain. Shakespeare's generation felt that this struggle had been victoriously concluded with Elizabeth. The history plays express a somewhat jingoistic nationalism, but also, in Shakespeare's plays at least, the passion for social order and the cautious political wisdom which were making England great. *Henry VI* is the crudest of Shakespeare's Histories; it gallops, with the speed of a boy's adventure story, from one high-pitched quarrel to the next. Yet one can find in it the beginnings of some of his great and lifelong themes.

The next Histories, *Richard III* and *King John,* and the comedy, *Love's Labor's Lost,* hardly belong to Shakespeare's apprenticeship. *Love's Labor's Lost* is particularly interesting: it was written, apparently, for the Court instead of the popular audience of the public theatres. It is a gently ironic picture of an aristocratic circle infatuated with neoplatonic notions of love and learning; and it shows that Shakespeare was already at home in the "best society," and in the fashionable literary humanism of the Renaissance.

As though all this were not enough, the young Shakespeare spent part of the years 1592-94, when the Plague made one of its descents upon London and the theatres were closed, writing his narrative poems, *Venus and Adonis, The Rape of Lucrece,* and *The Phoenix and the Turtle,* and perhaps some of the sonnets too. He dedicated *Venus and Adonis* to Southampton, the famous patron of the arts. It was immediately successful, and it made Shakespeare's reputation as a writer in circles where the theatre was not considered polite literature.

I have called this period "apprenticeship," but Shakespeare began to find himself almost at once. He was born with his genius for theatrical story-telling, and also that easy sympathy with men and ideas which enabled him to share the life of his times at every point. He had, above all, the ability to learn from his own playwrighting experience. Before 1594 he was already rethinking his discoveries, thereby swiftly deepening both his vision and his art.

II. Growing Mastery: From 1594, when Shakespeare joined The Lord Chamberlain's Men, to 1599, when the Globe Theatre opened.

The Lord Chamberlain's Men, which Shakespeare joined in 1594, was the company of actor-managers with whom he was to work for the rest of his life. It was the best company in London, including Richard Burbage, soon to be recognized as England's leading actor; Heminge and Condell, who were to publish the First Folio of Shakespeare's plays after his death; and Will Kempe, the renowned comedian. Their patron, the Lord Chamberlain (Lord Hunsdon) was a member of the Queen's Privy Council, in charge of her household and all the entertainments. He did not support his players; their income came mostly from their large public audiences. But he lent them the prestige of the Crown, defended them from the officials of the City of London (who had a bourgeois and puritanical mistrust of the theatre), and arranged for their frequent and well-paid appearances at Court. In addition to regular performances in the public theatres and at Court, The Lord Chamberlain's Men toured the provinces in the summer, and sometimes at other seasons also, when the Plague forced the closing of the City theatres.

In 1596 Shakespeare's only son, Hamnet, died in Stratford at the age of eleven. In 1597 he bought New Place, the largest house in Stratford, evidence that he was making a good living, and also that he continued to think of himself as a resident of his native town.

He wrote the following plays in approximately this period: *Romeo and Juliet; Richard II; Henry IV*, Parts 1 and 2; *The Merchant of Venice; A Midsummer Night's Dream; The Merry Wives of Windsor; Much Ado about Nothing; Henry V; As You Like It;* and perhaps *Twelfth Night.*

These are the plays of the most popular playwright of the day: Shakespeare was giving his public what it wanted. But he was also unfolding, through the popular tales he dramatized, his own intimate sense of human life. The plays may be classified as Comedies, Histories, and Tragedies, but each one is unique. They owe more to Shakespeare's own flexible art than they do to the theatrical conventions he inherited.

Richard II and *Henry IV*, Parts 1 and 2, are freer and deeper in language, in their rather disillusioned political wisdom, and above all in their character-drawing, than the early Histories. By the time he wrote *Henry V* Shakespeare seems to have tired of the History play, tied as it was to familiar events and to the immediate issues of politics. In the next phase he will turn from literal history to the freer and deeper form of tragedy.

The comedies of this period, the "Golden Comedies," are far more original in form and spirit than the "plotty" Latin farces of his apprenticeship. The titles and subtitles (*As You Like It*, or *Twelfth Night, Or What You Will*, for instance) suggest that Shakespeare was meeting a public demand for more plays like *A Midsummer Night's Dream*. But at the same time he was exploring an inspiration of his own. He had learned to combine several stories of different kinds in such a way as to suggest, in each play, a single poetic and ruefully smiling vision of human life. He presents the delusions of youth as fond and charming; he stages them in the light of dream, or of some brief festive occasion. The only exception is *The Merry Wives*, a farce which he may have written at the Queen's request.

The Merchant of Venice and *Romeo and Juliet* are akin in spirit to the comedies, but each represents also a new discovery. *The Merchant* is Shakespeare's first serious play about a commercial republic, and his first ambitious experiment in allegory. *Romeo and Juliet* brings into the theatre, for the first time, the themes, the music, and even the verse-forms of a very old tradition in European love-poetry, and in its structure foreshadows the great tragedies of the next phase.

In these intense five years Shakespeare's genius was coming into its own, and one can see its growth in every aspect of his complex art. His fabulous gift is most evident, perhaps, in the great characters that suddenly people his stage. Harry and Falstaff in *Henry IV*, Shylock in *The Merchant*, the Nurse in *Romeo*, Beatrice and Benedick in *Much Ado*, must have surprised even their author. One can see that Shakespeare's imagination was fed by the lively types that swarmed around him in London, and also by the actors whom he knew so well in his own company. A working theatre is a small society in itself, analogous to the larger human world around it. One can often feel, in the many-sided humanity of Shakespeare's characters—their fatness or leanness, their tricks of speech, life-rhythms that express certain temperaments—the presence of flesh-and-blood actors who would perform them. Perhaps Shakespeare's creations owe as much to his acting-company as to the stories he used. Yet in the long run they live with the life of Shakespeare's poetic imagination, which is more intense than any direct mimicry could be.

> *III. Maturity: The years of the great tragedies, from the acquisition of the Globe Theatre in 1599 to the acquisition of the Blackfriars' Theatre in 1608.*

In 1599 The Lord Chamberlain's Men acquired the illustrious Globe Theatre, which they were to occupy for the rest of Shakespeare's life. Elizabeth died in 1603, and James I ascended the throne. Fortunately James was as fond of the theatre as Elizabeth had been. He made The Lord Chamberlain's Men "The King's Men," thus taking Shakespeare's company under his royal patronage, and recognizing it as the finest in London. The King's Men seem to have enjoyed almost unbroken success, for they played often at Court and continued to attract large audiences at the Globe.

Shakespeare wrote the following plays in this period of eight or nine years: *Julius Caesar; Hamlet; All's Well That Ends Well; Troilus and Cressida; Measure for Measure; Othello; King Lear; Macbeth; Antony and Cleopatra; Timon of Athens; Coriolanus.*

The list looks to succeeding generations like a unique but natural miracle, a Sequoia Forest of the human spirit. No one has succeeded in mapping it satisfactorily, and every new reader is free to enjoy and explore it as his own understanding slowly grows.

Many attempts have been made to "explain" Shakespeare's tragic phase as the result of circumstances in his own life. We know that Hamnet, his only son, died in 1596, his father in 1601, and his mother in 1608. The last years of Queen Elizabeth's reign were darkened by trouble at home and abroad, especially her long quarrel with Essex. James's reign too, after a brief period of hopefulness, was filled with the beginnings of disorder. All over Europe the end of the Renaissance was a time of confusion and frightening premonitions of change. All of this, and probably more intimate experiences of which we know nothing, must have been grist to Shakespeare's mill. But the crucial question, how experience is transmuted into tragic poetry, is unanswerable.

The most illuminating studies are based on the plays themselves, and their relationships to earlier work, for Shakespeare (like other great artists) learned continually by rethinking his own achievements. It has been pointed out that some of the tragic characters grew, by mysterious processes of transformation and combination, out of their predecessors: Hamlet from Richard II, Brutus, Romeo; Macbeth from Richard III, perhaps Bolingbroke in *Richard II* and *Henry IV*. Shakespeare's mature mastery of versification, and also of form and plot, were the outcome of long practice; the musical harmony of imagery and symbol in a late play like *Antony and Cleopatra* was the fruit of years of writing. About the turn of the century the varied elements fell into place, and Shakespeare began to enjoy his full mastery.

The tragedies proper, especially *Hamlet, King Lear,* and *Macbeth,* which have to do with the tragic paradoxes of kingship, may be thought of as deeper mutations of the Histories. Like the Histories, these three plays picture the kind of society that Shakespeare knew and loved best, that of the Tudor monarchy. But Hamlet's Denmark, Lear's ancient Britain, and Macbeth's Scotland are not literally contemporary England. The stories of those plays are not, like the Histories, connected with familiar political struggles. Intimate as they are in detail, immediate though their life is—and instantly convincing—they have at the same time a certain legendary distance. They are mirrors in which Shakespeare could freely reflect the universal meanings he had found in his own and his country's experience.

The Roman tragedies, *Julius Caesar* and *Coriolanus,* are also derived from the Histories, but the Roman setting gives them a different quality. The characters and many details in these plays are Tudor English, but there is no doubt that Shakespeare wished them to evoke ancient Rome. Rome and its history had haunted the imagination of Europe since the dark ages, and Shakespeare's imagination since his schooldays; but he did not love Rome as he loved (and sometimes despaired of) his own monarchical society. He sees the fate of a Brutus or a Coriolanus in a colder and harder human world; between the mob one way and the wise but helpless philosophy of a Menenius, or the rationalizations of Brutus himself, the other way. In short, Rome, or the legendary idea of Rome, gave him another mirror in which to reflect another aspect of his tragic vision. And *Othello* reflects it in still another context. Set (like *The Merchant of Venice* and *Timon of Athens*) in a commercial republic, it is Shakespeare's most modern or "domestic" tragedy, foreshadowing Ibsen's well-made drama of individualism.

Even if one thinks only of the plays properly called "Tragedies," one can see that Shakespeare's sense of human destiny had not only deepened but widened, and now included most of the forms of human life and society visible at that time, the threshold of the modern world. But what are we to say of the other plays in the list? *Antony and Cleopatra*, for all its mortal sadness, hardly feels "tragic"; it floats like a dream, a transfiguration of the Golden Comedies. *Measure for Measure*, akin both to *Hamlet* and *The Tempest*, is a self-conscious political and theological allegory. *Troilus and Cressida*, conceived perhaps as a gigantic farce, has come to seem, since the early 'thirties, a prophetic picture of our own faithless "wars and lecheries." And so on. We cannot hope to grasp all of the aspects of Shakespeare's vision as it unfolded in these years, to say nothing of holding them all together.

But we can safely say that, just as the facts show that he was enjoying brilliant professional success, so the plays show "success" in a more intimate sense. The human creature must have appeared to him in an appalling light: "We that are young/ Shall never see so much, or live so long." But when we read the plays and hear their music, we are reminded that the tragic emotion includes exaltation. To have faced and then projected the tragic vision in poetry was a triumph of spirit. Shakespeare completed the great labors of his maturity in undiminished strength. Then he went on to digest the tragic vision in its turn, placing it in the serener perspective of the end of his life in the theatre.

> *IV. Synthesis and Serenity: From the acquisition of the Blackfriars' Theatre in 1608 to Shakespeare's death in Stratford in 1616.*

The King's Men bought the Blackfriars' Theatre in 1608, and thereafter used it regularly, in bad weather, in addition to their Globe Theatre. Blackfriars' was so called because it was in one of the monasteries which had been taken over by the Crown under Henry VIII. It was an indoor theatre, and had been used for some years by a company of boy-actors. The influence of its indoor stage can be seen in Shakespeare's last plays; and the increasing use of indoor stages from this time onward prepared the evolution of the modern theatre. The "Inn-yard theatres," like the Globe, for which most of Shakespeare's plays were written, were soon to disappear.

The purchase of Blackfriars' is one of several signs that Shakespeare was ending his theatrical career in comfort and prosperity. Some time after 1610 he began, probably gradually, to retire from active work in the theatre, and his last days were spent in his house, New Place, in Stratford. His bequests, including the famous one of his "second-best bed" to his wife, reveal a very substantial citizen of his native town. His small legacies to fellow members of The King's Men show his respect and affection for his lifelong colleagues; and the preface which Heminge and Condell wrote for their First Folio of his plays shows that they continued to revere him eight years after his death. Shakespeare's company must have possessed some rare virtues in addition to their talent, for The King's Men lasted longer than any theatre group in the English-speaking world, before or since. And Shakespeare's art owes a great deal to the acting ensemble for which he wrote.

He completed the following plays in this period: *Pericles; Cymbeline; The Winter's Tale; The Tempest;* and *Henry VIII.*

Henry VIII completes Shakespeare's chronicle of English history with the auspicious birth of Elizabeth, but it is a pageant and an allegory, rather than a History like the earlier plays which are so called. It is more interesting to the modern reader for the indirect light it sheds on Shakespeare's politics than as a play in its own right.

The other four plays, which were written in the order in which they are listed above, represent the harmonious end of Shakespeare's career. They are not tragedies, but theatre-poetry with subtle and manifold allegorical meanings. Each of their stories covers a whole generation, from childhood to age, instead of a single profound crisis like the stories of the tragedies. They are full of echoes of the earlier themes, as though Shakespeare were looking back over the course of his life and art. *The Tempest* is the last, the richest, and the most assured masterpiece of the four. Miranda and Ferdinand give us again the music of youth and its brave new world; the usurping Duke, with his treacheries, reminds us of the themes of guilt and suffering in the Histories and Tragedies. All these figures—and Caliban and Ariel and Gonzago and the rest—are lovingly brooded over by the Magician, Prospero, now ready to renounce the glorious cares of art and rule. It is natural to see Prospero as an image of Shakespeare, and the play as his own last word on the form and meaning of his own career, a detached but moving reflection of life from the cradle to the grave. Such a reading confirms the impression one gets from the sequence of Shakespeare's plays, and from the known facts of his life: that, more than any other man, he knew and gratefully accepted the mysterious experience of everyman.

Shakespeare did not impress his contemporaries as a spectacular personality, though many of them knew he was the foremost dramatist of that, or perhaps any, age. Ben Jonson, in the verses he wrote to go with the portrait in the First Folio, speaks for all who attempt to picture Shakespeare:

To the Reader.

This Figure, that thou here seest put,
   It was for gentle Shakespeare cut:
Wherein the Graver had a strife
   with Nature, to out doo the life:
O, could he but have drawne his wit
   As well in brasse, as he hath hit
His face, the Print would then surpasse
   All, that was ever writ in brasse.
But, since he cannot, Reader, looke
   Not on his Picture, but his Booke.

Shakespeare died in Stratford in 1616, at the unbelievably early age of fifty-two.

II. SHAKESPEARE'S THEATRE

Shakespeare wrote most of his plays for the Globe Theatre. He wrote also for the Court, the Inns of Court, and, toward the end of his career, for the indoor stage of the Black-friars' Theatre. But it was the Globe, its permanent acting-company, and its large public audiences, which chiefly determined the style of Shakespeare's dramaturgy. That theatre was Shakespeare's instrument, as important for his art as the orchestra available to a composer is for the music he writes.

Most of our knowledge of the Globe is derived from the contemporary sketch of the Swan—like the Globe, one of the "public theatres"—which is reproduced on page 175. Recent students of Shakespeare's theatre have made far more elaborate, and largely conjectural, reconstructions of the Globe. (For three of the most valuable studies, see "Suggestions for Further Reading," pp. 182-183.) The following simplified description refers to the accompanying sketch.

In the center, the stage-house, where the actors dressed and stored their costumes and properties, rises to a height of three stories, and is topped by the "hut," where the flag flies. In front of it the platform (five or six feet above the ground) projects into the "yard" where the groundlings stood. The yard is encircled by three roofed balconies, and there the richer members of the audience sat on cushioned seats. The yard and part of the platform are open to the sky. The façade of the stage-house has large double doors on either side, and the Globe had also a central opening (not shown in the sketch) equipped with curtains which could be closed, or opened to reveal an inner room. There is a large balcony at the second-story level; and the hut could be used for musicians, sound effects, and machinery. A roof, called "the heavens," supported on tall, ornate pillars, covers the upper stage; and there was a trapdoor in the platform leading down to the cellar or "hell," which could also be entered from inside the stage-house.

This theatre may strike us as primitive, but Shakespeare's contemporaries thought it rich and splendid. The interior was elaborately carved and painted, in a style like that of the allegorical archways erected in the London streets for James the First's coronation. For performances the stage would be hung with banners and tapestries, or, for a tragedy, with black. The actors were gorgeously and expensively costumed, and they used elaborate properties, not only "hand-props" like weapons and torches, but portable thrones, altars, and the like. They made frequent use of sound effects for thunder or the noise of battle. Music, a widely cultivated art at the time, was important. In Shakespeare's plays it was an essential element of his theatrical "orchestration." He used it to change the mood, to stress a rhythm, or to punctuate the movement of the story.

The stage of the Globe, complicated as it was, was a permanent setting entirely unlike the modern "picture-frame" stage. Realistic or illusory settings of the kind we know were impossible, and the permanently visible structure could not be changed. The light came from the sky, and the resources of modern lighting were undreamed of. The effect was to focus attention upon the actors and what they said. The Globe could accommodate two thousand spectators or more, but packed closely around three sides of the stage, they could follow the subtleties of the playing

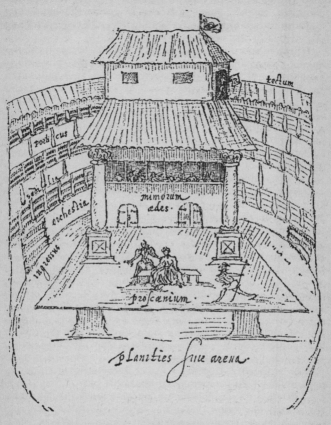

The Swan Theatre. Based on a drawing by Johannes
de Witt in Arend van Buchell's commonplace book.

like audiences in our "arena" theatres. The audience looked, perforce, to the actors, not only to create the characters, but also to build imaginatively, in word and deed, the changing scenes of the story.

There is every reason to believe that the actors in Shakespeare's company were up to their great task. The arts of language both written and spoken were carefully cultivated, in the schools and pulpits as well as in the theatre. Actors were expected not only to command the language, but to dance, sing, play musical instruments, and fence well enough to please the connoisseurs. Women's parts were taken by boys, also highly trained. They had often been choristers, accustomed to singing good and difficult music, or members of one of the children's theatres. According to some contemporary testimony, they were better than the actresses on the continent. The art of acting, indeed—as distinguished from type-casting or the exploitation of the actor's sex or personality—was apparently well understood. The actors were used to playing a great variety of roles, often several parts in one production. The great Burbage played such varied characters as Hamlet, Macbeth, and Othello. Shakespeare himself must have chosen him for these roles, or written the roles for him, which strongly suggests that he was an artist with a very flexible and reliable technique. Shakespeare himself was an actor, and the art of acting is at the very root of his whole playwrighting art. We must think of that company, not like the cast of a Broadway show, hastily assembled for four weeks' rehearsal, but as resembling one of the highly trained companies of modern Europe. It must have been, in short, an accomplished and experienced ensemble.

Shakespeare's unrealistic or make-believe theatre, with the skilled player on the nearly empty platform, gave the dramatic poet great imaginative freedom. Modern playwrights often envy this freedom, and seek it on the arena-stage or on the bare stage. Thornton Wilder's *Our Town*, for instance, counts entirely on the actors and the willing audience to establish the scenes of the play. But Shakespeare's theatre, in its very structure, placed the poet and

actors in the center, and so determined the style we know.
In the opening scene of *Hamlet* Shakespeare, with the aid
of two players, creates the night on the parapet in a matter
of seconds:

BARNARDO: 'Tis now struck twelve, get thee to bed
                Francisco.
FRANCISCO: For this relief much thanks, 'tis bitter cold,
                And I am sick at heart.
BARNARDO: Have you had quiet guard?
FRANCISCO: Not a mouse stirring.

Much of the sweep of Shakespeare's poetry, its power to
evoke scenes of many kinds and moods, is based on the col-
laboration between poet, actor, and audience in a theatre
where literal realism was impossible.

On that stage, moreover, Shakespeare was not limited to
a realistic time-scheme, or to detailed specifications of place.
He used both time and place, not for documentation, but as
means of conveying the action of the story. It is a mistake
to inquire (as many students have felt obliged to do) just
how many days or weeks Hamlet spent in England, or just
which room in the palace Cleopatra occupies at the moment; such information is irrelevant to the unfolding of the
play.

The stage of the Globe was, however, an extremely flexible instrument for suggesting changes of place where that
was essential. The main playing-area was no doubt the platform, but the stage-house façade offered many other possibilities for the make-believe of the players. The big doors
could be opened for the entrance of military processions,
funerals, or royal progresses. The balcony could represent a
castle-parapet, or Cleopatra's monument, or Juliet's bed-
room window. The central opening might be used as an
inner room, or its curtains might be suddenly opened to
reveal a special effect, a prepared "set-piece" like the armed
head, bloody child, and endless row of kings with which
the Witches startle Macbeth. Careful studies of recent years
have shown us how flexible that stage was. The clarity and
theatrical effectiveness of Shakespeare's plays is evident as

soon as one understands the stage for which he wrote them.

The traditional divisions of Shakespeare's plays into acts and scenes, with indications of place for every scene, were added by the long sequence of editors of the texts. The plays were originally played straight through, with no intermissions, and with only such suggestions of place as emerged from the play itself. The traditional labels of act, scene, and place are retained in this series to assist the reader (who does not have the benefit of Shakespeare's stage) to get his bearings. But to sense the rhythm which Shakespeare intended, one should think of the play as unfolding without a break from beginning to end.

One should also know something about what the theatre meant to Shakespeare's Londoners, for a theatre is partly the creation of its audience. The theatre was the Londoner's chief form of amusement, rivaled only by the bawdy-houses and the savage sport of bear-baiting. Everyone went to the theatre: the much-maligned groundlings who could stand in the yard and watch the show for a penny; law students, by all accounts a lively and intelligent group; the nobles and rich merchants, with their ladies; the " 'prentices," who have been described as clerks and young business people; in short, a cross-section of that great generation. They did not have our newspapers, magazines, movies, radio or television. Even books were much rarer and harder to get than they are now. The London theatre was a chief medium of public communication and an important instrument in the building of the common picture of man and his society. Holinshed and other recent Chroniclers were interpreting English history as leading up to Elizabeth's beloved reign; Roman history, Italian and French fiction, and old stories and legends of many kinds, were widely read; and narratives from all these sources were made to live again in the performances of the players. Hamlet must have expressed the common feeling when he called the players "abstracts and brief chronicles of the time." His definition of the purpose of playing suggests what the theatre meant then: "To hold, as 'twere, the mirror up to nature; to show virtue her own feature, scorn her own image, and the very age and body of the time his form and pressure."

The proud device which Shakespeare's company adopted for their Globe Theatre was Hercules lifting the sphere of the earth. There are many indications in Shakespeare's plays that he thought of his theatre's "wooden O" as a microcosm, a symbolic representation of man's world as that age conceived it. Burbage, playing Hamlet, could point to the platform on which he stood as "this goodly frame, the earth," which seemed to him, in his melancholy, "a sterile premontory." When he spoke of the heavens as "this majestical roof fretted with golden fire" he had the actual roof far above his head, which was in fact painted, probably with stars, signs of the zodiac, or allegorical figures. When he heard his father's ghost the sound came from the cellarage or "hell" under the platform. Thus Shakespeare used his stage, not only to present the immediate events of the story, but also the cosmic setting where man, crawling between heaven and earth, met his mysterious fate. The modern reader can enter the world of Shakespeare's poetry more easily, and with fuller understanding, if he remembers that the symbolic stage itself was a basis for it.

III. SHAKESPEARE ON THE MODERN STAGE

The Puritan Revolution put an end to the theatre as Shakespeare had known it in 1642, when Parliament prohibited all stage-plays. The Restoration reopened the theatres in 1660, but the players had moved indoors, and most of the public theatres that Shakespeare used were gone. D'Avenant and Killigrew revived Shakespeare's plays at once, but Shakespeare would hardly have recognized them. The understanding of his art had decayed along with the theatres in which it was formed.

D'Avenant began the practice of adapting and "improving" Shakespeare for the new theatre. He arranged the plays for the indoor stages of Restoration London, which were already beginning to resemble our proscenium-stages, dividing them into scenes which could be realistically or spectacularly set. He also drastically altered the texts to suit the taste of the new society. He cut or re-wrote passages which he found indelicate; he re-arranged plots to make them "clearer" or more moral; and he was quite willing to shift whole scenes from one play to another. Many of his bad habits governed the staging of Shakespeare almost to our own day. The barnstorming Shakespeareans whom our grandfathers saw in opera-houses all over this country were essentially within that tradition.

It was Granville-Barker, after William Poel, who did the most to free the staging of Shakespeare from its inherited encumbrances. He demonstrated in his own productions and in his famous *Prefaces to Shakespeare* that the plays—including those which had been thought literary and un-stageable—are extraordinarily clear and effective in the theatre, provided the director does not feel obliged to pause and set a realistic scene with every change of place. As the implications of Granville-Barker's views were worked out, the flexibility and imaginative scope of Shakespeare's stage-techniques became clearer and clearer to a new generation in the theatre.

Contemporary producers inherit this improved under-standing of Shakespeare's purely theatrical effectiveness. There is no longer any need to think that Shakespeare is hard to stage simply because realistic staging strangles him. Moreover our theatre is no longer limited to realism or heavy romantic spectacle. We are accustomed to perma-nent settings, arenas, bare stages, and other arrangements designed to secure for poet and performer the kind of freedom Shakespeare enjoyed. The modern producer is in a good position to understand Shakespeare's theatrical in-tentions, and he is free, after that, to consult his own taste —subject, of course, to the limitations imposed by his budget, his actors, and his audience.

If no standard form of Shakespeare-staging has emerged in our time, that is because the theatre itself is so varied. The productions we see, good and bad in different ways, reflect a bewildering variety of intentions. Modern dress may be used to stress the contemporaneity of a play like *Troilus;* productions like Copeau's use period music and costume for poetic purposes; *Coriolanus* or *Julius Caesar* may be pointed up in such a way as to bring out a fascist (or anti-fascist) thesis. Shakespeare is constantly adapted to the movies, television, radio, and dance and opera. In recent years off-Broadway, college, and community theatres have often staged Shakespeare "straight"—relying on the acting and directing, and spending very little on sets and costumes. Some of these productions have had great vitality and unexpected but convincing subtlety; probably they give the best sense of Shakespeare's own direct theatrical style.

There is room in our time for many interpretations of Shakespeare, both on and off the stage. The comments on separate plays in this series, written by well-known actors, directors, poets, and critics, are intended to suggest some of the living approaches to Shakespeare, and some of the meanings which his many-sided art has for us.

SUGGESTIONS FOR FURTHER READING

This short list is intended to assist the reader who wishes to inform himself further about Shakespeare in the light of modern studies. Most of the books referred to are easy to find in libraries or recent editions. Asterisks (*) indicate books available in paperbound editions.

Many of the books listed below contain bibliographies, and more detailed studies of particular plays are listed in the Introductions to this series.

I. SHAKESPEARE'S LIFE AND TIMES

*Chute, Marchette. *Shakespeare of London*. New York: 1956.

An excellent popular biography, containing the known facts without the usual uncertain speculations. Especially valuable for its careful accounts of Stratford, London, Shakespeare's theatres, and his colleagues and patrons.

Halliday, F. E. *Shakespeare: A Pictorial Biography*. New York: 1956.
   A short account of the known facts of Shakespeare's life and surroundings, profusely illustrated with photographs, prints, and other pictorial materials.

*Trevelyan, G. M. *History of England*. Volume II: The Tudors and the Stuart Era. New York: 1953.
   A short and readable account of English history in the time of Shakespeare.

Tillyard, E. M. W. *The Elizabethan World Picture*. New York: 1944.
   A description of the way man, his society, and his world looked in Shakespeare's time. It throws light on Shakespeare's theatre, which was a kind of model of the Elizabethan's "world," and on the background of his poetry.

*Fluchère, Henri. *Shakespeare and the Elizabethans,* with a Foreword by T. S. Eliot. New York: 1956.
   A recent and stimulating book on Shakespeare the dramatist, in relation to other Elizabethans, and to the times in which they lived.

*Eliot, T. S. *Essays on Elizabethan Drama*. New York: 1956.
   Brief essays which do not include Shakespeare, but the book is one of the most influential of recent years, and clearly illustrates the new interest in the poetry and drama of Shakespeare's age.

II. SHAKESPEARE IN THE THEATRE

Adams, John Cranford. *The Globe Playhouse: Its Design and Equipment*. New York: 1942.

Hodges, C. Walter. *The Globe Restored*. New York: 1954.

Smith, Irwin. *Shakespeare's Globe Playhouse. A Modern Reconstruction in Text and Scale Drawings.* New York: 1956.

Dr. Adams's book is the most elaborate recent effort to reconstruct Shakespeare's own theatre. It is based on painstaking scholarship, but many details are necessarily conjectural, and are questioned by other authorities. The other two books rely very much on Dr. Adams's, but differ in details. Mr. Smith is interested in the methods of actual construction in Shakespeare's time. Mr. Hodges' study is the shortest and most readable, and contains many well-chosen illustrations.

Granville-Barker, Harley. *Prefaces to Shakespeare.* Princeton: 1946.

The fundamental book on Shakespeare's plays as works for the theatre. Ten plays are discussed from the point of view of their staging as Shakespeare himself planned it. Granville-Barker was both an authority on Shakespeare's stage and a skilled director in the modern theatre.

De Banke, Cecile. *Shakespearean Production, Then and Now. A Manual for the Scholar Player.* New York: 1953.

Watkins, Ronald. *On Producing Shakespeare.* London: 1950.

*Webster, Margaret. *Shakespeare without Tears.* New York: 1957.

These three books are concerned with the modern staging of Shakespeare. Professor De Banke's is addressed primarily to the school or college director. Mr. Watkins is talking to professionals, and arguing for the necessity of understanding Shakespeare's own theatre-practice. Miss Webster speaks out of her wide experience as a producer of Shakespeare here and in England. Her book is useful also for those who wish only to read the plays.

III. CRITICISM AND INTERPRETATION

*Bradley, A. C. *Shakespearean Tragedy*. New York: 1955
  Bradley summarizes the best nineteenth century criticism, which emphasizes the creation of character. His book is one of the foundations for the modern understanding of Shakespeare. This volume is concerned primarily with *Hamlet, Othello, King Lear*, and *Macbeth*.

Goddard, Harold C. *The Meaning of Shakespeare*. Chicago: 1950.
  A stimulating reading of all of Shakespeare; a useful and provocative introduction.

*Traversi, D. A. *An Approach to Shakespeare*. New York: 1956.
  A short study by a well-known English critic who has taken account of recent developments in Shakespeare criticism.

*Van Doren, Mark. *Shakespeare*. New York: 1953.
  A reading of all of Shakespeare's works by a scholar who is also a sensitive lyric poet.

Clemen, W. H. *The Development of Shakespeare's Imagery*. Cambridge, Mass.: 1951.

Moulton, R. G. *Shakespeare as Dramatic Artist*. Oxford: 1929.

  These two books, which are somewhat technical, are concerned with Shakespeare's art as a writer of plays. Clemen's book may serve as an introduction to the many recent studies of Shakespeare's poetry. Moulton's is still the best analysis of Shakespeare's methods in constructing his plots.

Shakespeare Criticism: A Selection. Smith, D. N., editor. Oxford: 1916.

Shakespeare Criticism, 1919-1935. Selected with an Introduction by Anne Bradby. Oxford: 1936.

Shakespeare: Modern Essays in Criticism. Dean, Leonard F., editor. New York: 1957.

>These three books constitute a useful sampling of the vast literature of Shakespeare criticism from his own time to ours.

IV. REFERENCE BOOKS

The New Variorum Shakespeare. H. H. Furness and H. H. Furness, editors. Philadelphia: 1878–.

>Most of Shakespeare's more important plays have appeared in this series, which is being continued by a committee of the Modern Language Association. It contains exhaustive notes on textual problems, many critical comments, and some sources.

The First Folio of Shakespeare's Plays, in a Facsimile Edition. Helge Kokeritz and Charles Tyler Prouty, editors. New Haven: 1955.

>The facsimile of the First Folio, published originally by Shakespeare's colleagues, is harder to read than a modern edition; but the old spelling and punctuation give valuable insights into Shakespeare's language.

C. J. Sisson. *New Readings in Shakespeare*. Two Vols. Cambridge: 1956.

>The latest authoritative survey of the problems of Shakespeare's text, with an illuminating essay on modern methods of textual analysis, by the textual editor of this series.

A Shakespeare Glossary. C. T. Onions, editor. Oxford: 1919.

A New and Complete Concordance or Verbal Index to Words, Phrases, and Passages in the Dramatic Works of Shakespeare. John Bartlett, compiler. New York: 1894.

Chambers, E. K. *The Elizabethan Stage*. Four Vols. Oxford: 1923.

Chambers, E. K. *William Shakespeare: A Study of Facts and Problems*. Oxford: 1930.

> The two works of Chambers are a mine of information, and the foundation of a great deal of modern Shakespeare scholarship.

Bentley, G. E. *The Jacobean and Caroline Stage*. Five Vols. Oxford: 1941-56.
> This is the standard work on the English stage. It carries Chambers' work, which ends with the death of Shakespeare, to the closing of the theatres. Volumes I and II are devoted to "Dramatic Companies and Players," Volumes III, IV, and V to "Plays and Playwrights."

Shakespeare's England: An Account of the Life and Manners of His Age. Two Vols. Oxford: 1916.
> A collection of essays by experts in various fields, planned by the late Sir Walter Raleigh. Very useful as background for the plays.

Ralli, Augustus. *A History of Shakespeare Criticism*. Two Vols. Oxford: 1932.

Odell, George C. D. *Shakespeare from Betterton to Irving*. Two Vols. New York: 1920.
> A history of Shakespeare productions since the Restoration.

A Companion to Shakespeare Studies. Granville-Barker, Harley, and Harrison, G. B., editors. New York: 1934.
> Essays by leading authorities on Shakespeare's life, theatre, poetry, and sources, and on scholarly and critical problems. Useful in itself and as a guide to further study.

Ebisch, Walther, and Schucking, L. L. *A Shakespeare Bibliography*. Oxford: 1931.

———— Supplement for the Years 1930-1935. Oxford: 1937.

Glossary

This glossary, based on the glossary prepared by Hilda Hulme for the *Complete Works of Shakespeare* edited by C. J. Sisson, was made especially for *The Taming of the Shrew* by H. H. Smith. Unfamiliar words, names, foreign phrases, and English words used in unfamiliar senses are defined here. Words which may easily be found in any standard modern dictionary are generally not included.

abandoned: banished.

Adonis: a young man loved unsuccessfully by Venus. He was killed by a boar through the jealousy of Mars.

Aeacides: descendants of Aeacus, a son of Jupiter.

affied: betrothed.

aglet-baby: a metal tag in the shape of a small figure.

Ajax: Greek hero of the Trojan war.

Alcides: Hercules.

amort: dejected.

Anna: sister of Dido, Queen of Carthage.

arras counterpoint: tapestry counterpane.

awful: reverential, awe-inspiring.

baccarè: get back.

basta: enough.

bate: to flutter the wings ready for flight.

bears more: is nearer.

be-mete: to measure, measure out punishment to.

bemoiled: covered with mud.

ben venuto: welcome.

bestraught: distracted.

bots: parasitic worms or maggots.

bottom: bobbin.

brach: bitch.

brave: adj., finely dressed, splendid; n., insult; v., to insult.

breeching: liable to be whipped.

buckler: shield.

bug: bogey, terror.

burthen: refrain.

cart: to punish as a prostitute.

chapeless: without a sheath.

clapped up: agreed on.

cock's: God's.

coffin: a pastry mold for a pie.

comonty: comedy.

con tutto il cuore, ben trovato: with all my heart, well met.

conster: construe.

continency: temperance, restraint.

cony-catch: to cheat.

copatain: high-crowned.

crack-hemp: one likely to be hanged.

crupper: the strap of leather reaching from the saddle to the tail of a horse.

cullion: low wretch.

curst: ill-tempered, malignant.

Cytherea: Venus, the goddess of love.

Daphne: nymph loved by Apollo; to preserve her chastity, she was changed into a laurel tree by the gods.

denier: French coin of little value.

descry: to see.

Dian: Diana, goddess of chastity and the hunt.

diaper: towel.

embossed: swollen, foaming at the mouth.

farthingale: hooped petticoat.

fashions: a disease of the skin in horses.

fault: lost scent.

fives: strangles, a disease of horses.

Florentius: had to find the answer to the question "What do women most desire?" An ugly old woman promised him an answer if he would marry her. After marriage she became beautiful.

forthcoming: ready to appear in court.

fret: stop of a stringed instrument. *fretting:* wearing away.

fustian: coarse cloth.

galliass: large galley.

gamut: musical scale.

gaud: plaything, showy ornament.

gird: joke.

glanders: disease of horses, characterized by discharge of sticky matter from the nose.

gogs-wouns: God's wounds.

haggard: female hawk difficult to tame because caught in maturity.

half-cheeked: with a piece

missing or broken on one side.

hap: fortune, chance; to happen.

haply: perhaps.

heavy: sad.

hilding: good-for-nothing person.

hipped: lame in the hip.

hold: endure, remain solid; to bet.

holidame: holiness.

humour: fancy, idea.

in a few: briefly.

indifferent: equally.

Io: maiden loved by Jupiter.

jack: quarter of a pint.

jade: horse of poor condition or vicious temper.

jealous: suspicious, doubtful.

jointure: part of a dowry reserved for a widow.

jolthead: blockhead.

Jove: ruler of the gods.

junket: delicacy.

kersey: coarse cloth.

kindly: according to nature.

lampass: disease of horses in which flesh swells behind front teeth.

Leda's daughter: Helen of Troy.

leet: special court held by lord of a manor.

link: torch, lampblack

list: selvage, band.

loss: loss of scent.

Lucrece: a Roman matron and pattern of virtue who killed herself after being raped by Sextus Tarquinius.

malt-horse: brewer's horse.

meacock: coward, weakling.

mercatant: merchant.

mew up: imprison.

Minerva: goddess of wisdom.

minion: favorite, darling, harlot.

mi perdonato: pardon me.

mose in the chine: to suffer from glanders.

near-legged before: with forelegs close together.

neat: calf.

nill: will not.

on the score: in debt.

packing: plotting.

pantaloon: foolish old man in the Commedia dell'Arte.

parle: converse.

passing: exceedingly.

paucas pallabris: few words.

peat: spoiled girl.

pedascule: schoolmate, pedant.

Pegasus: the winged horse ridden by Bellerophon.

pheeze: to drive away.

point: lace for attaching hose to doublet.

policy: statecraft, trickery.

port: bearing, state.

prefer: recommend.

rate: to value, to scold.

rayed: fouled, dirtied.

rebused: used for abused.

redime te captum quam queas minimo: buy yourself out of captivity for as little as you can.

road: harbor.

roundly: directly.

rudesby: rough, unmannerly person.

Semiramis: wife of Ninus, mythical founder of the Assyrian empire.

sessa: probably a cry used to encourage hounds.

Sibyl: prophetess of Cumae, to whom Apollo granted as many years of life as there were grains in a handful of sand.

skipper: flighty youth.

sop: anything saturated with liquor.

spavins: disease of horses consisting of swelling of joints.

specialty: contract under seal.

sped: done away with.

speed: to fare, to be successful.

stale: bait, prostitute, laughing stock.

stand: to oppose.

stead: to be of use to, to help.

stock: person without feeling.

stomach: appetite; pride, anger.

supposes: expectations, pretenses.

third-borough: constable.

turn: requirements.

uncase: undress.

unpinked: not pierced with eyelet holes, not patterned or scalloped.

vail: to humble.

welkin: sky.

white: bull's eye, with a pun on the name "Bianca."

winded: sounded.

windgalls: a soft tumor on a horse's leg.

Xanthippe: wife of Socrates, famous for her shrewishness.

yellows: jaundice.

A NOTE ON THE GENERAL EDITOR

After completing three years at Oxford on a Rhodes Scholarship, Francis Fergusson was Assistant Director of the American Laboratory Theatre for four years. He has taught at the New School for Social Research, Bennington College, and Indiana University, was a member of the Institute for Advanced Study at Princeton University, and director of the Princeton Seminars in Literary Criticism. He is now University Professor of Comparative Literature at Rutgers. Professor Fergusson is the author of The Idea of a Theatre, Dante's Drama of the Mind, *and* The Human Image in Dramatic Literature.

A NOTE ON THE TYPE AND LAYOUT

The Laurel Shakespeare is composed in Times Roman, an unusually clear and readable type face. Its qualities of compactness make possible a larger size of type than that used in most editions of Shakespeare past and present. The text of the plays has been arranged with the names of the speakers on separate lines; this is the arrangement generally used in the professional theatre for acting scripts as well as reading versions. The line numbers of The Laurel Shakespeare are those of the Globe Edition of 1864; these line numbers are the ones used for reference by almost all Shakespearean critics.

Other distinguished Laurel Editions available in 1958

SHORT STORY MASTERPIECES   75¢
Robert Penn Warren and Albert Erskine, editors

4 PLAYS BY SHAW. *The Devil's Disciple,*   50¢
Candida, Caesar and Cleopatra, Captain
Brassbound's Conversion

GREAT AMERICAN SHORT STORIES   50¢
Wallace and Mary Stegner, editors

GREAT ENGLISH SHORT STORIES   50¢
Christopher Isherwood, editor

GREAT RUSSIAN SHORT STORIES   50¢
Norris Houghton, editor

GREAT ITALIAN SHORT STORIES   50¢
P. M. Pasinetti, editor

For publication after 1958

GREAT ORIENTAL SHORT STORIES   50¢
Yukio Mishima, editor

GREAT GERMAN SHORT STORIES   50¢
Stephen Spender, editor

GREAT RUSSIAN SHORT NOVELS   50¢

If these books cannot be obtained locally, send price
plus 5¢ for postage and handling for each copy to
Dell Publishing Co., 321 West 44th Street, New
York 36, N. Y. If order is for five or more copies,
no postage or handling charge is necessary.